PARENT-TEACHER COLLECTION

PARENTS ARE TEACHERS, TOO

ENRICHING YOUR CHILD'S FIRST SIX YEARS

CLAUDIA JONES

🐺 **WILLIAMSON PUBLISHING CO.** CHARLOTTE, VERMONT 05445

Library of Congress
Cataloging-in-Publication Data

Jones, Claudia.
   Parents are teachers, too.

   Bibliography: p.
   1. Child rearing.   2. Education, Preschool—Parent
participation.   I. Title.
HQ769.J752   1988   649'.1   87-37246
ISBN 0-913589-35-7

Cover and interior design: Trezzo-Braren Studio
Cover photograph: Jack Williamson
Photography: Marcy Nassikas
Typography: Villanti & Sons, Printers, Inc.
Printing: Capital City Press

Williamson Publishing Co.
Charlotte, Vermont 05445

Manufactured in the United States of America

10 9 8 7 6 5 4 3 2

With special appreciation to Marcy Nassikas and the
children of West Wind Montessori School, Charlotte,
Vermont, as well as Linda, Ashley, Ryan, and Whitney
Williamson; Barbara Garlough, Hank Moore, Peter
Guyton, Lisa Lynn.

CONTENTS

PREFACE

9   1   WHO, ME? A TEACHER?

23   2   YOUR CHILD'S SELF-ESTEEM

37   3   DEVELOPING SKILLS FOR LEARNING

45   4   DEVELOPING A LOVE OF READING

57   5   LEARNING TO READ

83   6   BEGINNING TO PRINT

91   7   LANGUAGE: HAVING FUN WITH WORDS

103   8   MATH: SO MUCH MORE THAN COUNTING!

119   9   DEVELOPING MUSCLES, COORDINATION, AND "GOOD SPORTS"

133   10   CREATIVE THINKING

141   11   ENCOURAGING YOUR CHILD'S CURIOSITY

149   12   NURTURING ARTISTIC EXPRESSION

157   13   SINGERS, DANCERS, AND MUSIC MAKERS

161   14   WHAT ABOUT TELEVISION?

167   15   SUMMER: DEALING WITH "MOM, WHAT CAN I DO?"

179   16   ENTERING KINDERGARTEN

BIBLIOGRAPHY

APPENDIX

> *To my parents, for giving me a love of learning,*
> *To my husband, for encouraging me to begin and*
> *continue my writing, and*
> *To my son, for giving this book real meaning for me.*

Rights & Permissions

Williamson Publishing Company and Claudia Jones gratefully acknowledge the granting of permission to quote, reference, and/or reprint from the following publications: "A Developmental Sequence For Teaching Social Behaviors," by R.S. Neel and S. Winslow, *Pointer*, 20 (2); *A Father Reads To His Children* by Orville Prescott, E.P. Dutton, 1965; *Help Your Child Learn To Read* by Harry Forgan, The Pagurian Corporation Ltd, Toronto, Canada, 1975; *The Hurried Child: Growing Up Too Fast Too Soon* by David Elkind, Addison-Wesley Publishing Co., 1981; *Learning for Little Kids* by Sandy Jones, article by Raymond Stinar, Houghton Mifflin Co., 1978; *Learning for Little Kids* by Sandy Jones, illustration by Sally L. Wright, Houghton-Mifflin Co., 1978; *The Lewiston (ID) Morning Tribune*; *The Literary Hoax* by Paul Copperman, William Morrow & Co., 1978; *Mr. Rogers Talks With Parents* by Fred Rogers with Barry Head, Berkeley Publishing Corporation, 1983; *A Parent's Guide To Children's Reading* by Nancy Larrick, Doubleday & Co., 1958; *The Read-Aloud Handbook* by Jim Trelease, Penguin Books, 1985; *Redbook*, article by Connie Broughton, May, 1982; *Redbook*, article by Cherie Taylor Pedersen, July, 1982; "Roadblock: A Game to Make Frustration Fun" by R.S. Neel, *Teaching Exceptional Children* (1); *The Semantic Organizer Approach To Writing and Reading Instruction*, by Pehrsson/Robinson, Aspen Publishers, Inc., 1985; *Your Child's Self-Esteem*, by Dorothy Corkille Briggs, Doubleday & Co., 1970.

Acknowledgements

This book would not exist if, back in 1980, the management of the *Lewiston Morning Tribune* of Lewiston, Idaho, had not taken a chance on something new—a weekly column encouraging parents to become involved in their children's education. I am grateful for their shared belief in my goal. To Bill Thompson, the editor with whom I worked most closely, I owe special thanks for four years of patience and encouragement.

My column would not have endured if it had not been for the many wonderfully supportive and positive letters I received from readers. I am indebted to them for their enthusiasm and the "desire for more" which gave me the boost I needed to continue to seek out new ideas and activities.

I also owe a great deal to my book editor, Susan Williamson, who, by looking at my manuscript from the reader's standpoint, was able to offer invaluable suggestions for its improvement. Her encouragement and guidance have made this book stronger and more effective than I imagined possible.

There are others to whom I am extremely grateful:

—To Loretta Stowers, Karen Smith, Holly Abel, Terri Maurer and the others who taught with me at Culdesac School and shared ideas, suggested topics, and offered materials for my columns.

—To all of my students. In addition to making going to work each day a genuine pleasure, they provided me with the inspiration for countless columns and helped test many new ideas and activities.

—To Polly Hoff for the majority of the illustrations included in this book.

—To Nita Hughes and Doris Truett for their help in getting my manuscript typed and printed at different stages of its development.

PREFACE

When my husband and I moved to Idaho, I left behind a job teaching sixth grade in a team situation with an extremely dedicated teacher and good friend. Unable to find a teaching position during that first school year, I wondered how I might somehow keep my hand in education. How could I teach without a classroom of students?

My husband, recalling an earlier attempt I'd made at writing a magazine article for parents, suggested that I propose a column along the same lines to the newspaper. The editor liked the idea, and although I started teaching again the next fall, I continued to write my column, offering ideas to parents who wanted to take an active part in their children's education.

I received many, many letters from readers of my column assuring me that my suggestions were helpful. Some said they clipped the columns from the paper to save for future reference. It is because of this supportive reaction from my readers that I believe a book of the same material will benefit interested parents, step-parents, and adult friends of preschool and elementary age children.

If you feel excited about helping your child develop into an intelligent and caring human being, if you are willing to spend time with him, and if you are searching for practical ideas on preparing your child for and introducing him to academics, this book can be a great help to you.

Parents Are Teachers, Too is not meant to be read straight through. I hope that you will read Chapters 1 and 2 first, carefully considering the ideas presented and questions raised. I would suggest you then read through the introductory portion of each of the other chapters, familiarizing yourself with the ideas involved and the activities which follow.

When it seems appropriate, you can then turn back to a particular chapter and, with your child, work on an activity *as it suits you.*

You might want to set aside a certain time each day or a certain evening each week for your special time together. Or you may want to pull the book out and work on an activity when you suddenly find yourself free of other obligations. *If you make it an enjoyable activity, a special treat for you, the time will be special for your child as well.*

Work only as long as it remains enjoyable. This will be 15 minutes or less for most activities. If you come upon a new and difficult concept, don't keep at it until you both become totally frustrated. That would defeat the purpose of your time together. You can always go back to the task at another time. One thing to keep in mind: *It is better to work for short periods of time, more often, than to work for long periods of time, less often.*

Where sets of activities are not numbered, the order in which you try them is not important. Numbered activities are listed, as much as possible, from least difficult to most difficult, although there is no hard and fast rule saying that a child must be able to do #1 before you try #2. Past experiences and individual differences will account for some children being able to do #7 before they can do #4. Most activities can be made more or less difficult, depending on your child's capabilities.

Few of the activities suggested involve sitting at a table with pencil and paper. Rather, these activities are to be used in free moments in the car or out in the yard, or as play activities. They can fill otherwise "lost" moments that come during the quiet time on a hot summer's day, while standing in the check-out line at the supermarket, sitting in the doctor's office, or waiting for dinner to be ready.

Parents Are Teachers, Too is meant to give you ideas, to get you thinking in terms of "What could I help my child experience from this moment, from this activity?" You want to ask questions which require more than a yes or no answer. You want to help your child learn to think creatively and critically, to exercise his brain and, very importantly, to enjoy the process.

Parents Are Teachers, Too is also meant to help you introduce your child to a number of fundamental skills—both academic and nonacademic. By helping him practice these skills at home, you will increase your child's chances of developing to his potential. By providing him opportunities to *experience*, rather than just observe, you will make learning more meaningful. Your involvement will give not only his education, but also his self-confidence, a terrific boost.

If there are some topics which you think you might be uncomfortable teaching (about which you think, "Oh, I was never good at that!"), I hope you will read through those chapters anyway. I think you will find there is a lot more that you do know and can explain to your child than you may have realized. Also, take the opportunity to learn along with your child in an area where you feel "lacking"; that is perhaps the best example you can set—showing your own desire to learn, and that learning never ends.

The reward for all your effort will come in those moments when you are with your child and his eyes sparkle with delight as he learns something new. "Oh, I get it!" You will feel tremendous satisfaction when you watch your child with other children, and see him share a cookie or hear him yell, "Good try!" To witness all the steps of your child's growth, realizing how normal and necessary each step is, is in itself a rich experience.

Enjoy the book, the glow of positive learning, the experience of parenting. Most of all, enjoy your child!

Claudia Jones

Note: For reasons of simplicity, I refer to the child in the masculine throughout the book. No sexism is intended. I simply find writing "he or she" or "s/he" distracting and cumbersome. Teachers, on the other hand, I refer to in the feminine, which in preschool and elementary school is still the case more often than not.

WHO, ME A TEACHER?

The Family

One Sunday afternoon I spent a few hours at the public swimming pool at Washington State University. One family in particular caught my eye. The mother sat by the pool with her 6-week-old son, while the father was in the water with the two older daughters. The 7-year-old swam off with other children, feeling very much at home in the water, leaving the father to focus his attention on the 3-year-old.

When I first began to watch, they were playing in the water, the father on occasion dunking his daughter. She would come up grinning and laughing, loving every minute of it. A little while later, I observed the father and daughter on the diving board. They jumped off together, daughter in her father's arms. Not long afterwards, I watched the two jump off the board again, but this time they held hands. No longer were Dad's protective arms around his daughter. Before I left that afternoon, the father no longer got out of the pool. The daughter walked alone to the end of the diving board and jumped into the outstretched arms of her father several feet below.

From the side of the pool, the mother expressed her excitement and pride. Not only did the mother cheer her 3-year-old on, but she took time to draw the attention of the older daughter to her younger sister's progress. Sharing the excitement of accomplishment, the situation became a family affair. As a family, these people had learned to support, trust and encourage each other.

Such sharing creates a special cohesiveness in a family. It requires time and effort to look for and recognize opportunities for sharing, and the results are not something which can be measured. They can only be felt inside.

Knowing one's family is there to offer support, encouragement, and sympathy when needed, allows a child to venture out from the family unit. He can take chances, test out his independence, become a person in his own right, and still know that he has a haven where he will be accepted no matter what. In the safety of his family, he can express his hopes and apprehensions without fear of humiliation. He can learn to be a caring person, one with feelings he can admit to and understand.

Any energy and time that you expend sitting and talking with your child, playing a game, learning new things, watching the stars, is that much more insurance that you will both become more complete human beings, happy with your own lives, and understanding the lives of those around you.

Why Not Leave Education to the Schools?

Parents can leave it to the schools to teach their child to read or count or write his name. They can let their child start school not knowing how to skip or hit a baseball. But a child's best educational opportunities and future growth depend on the combined effort of parent, teacher, and student. *The greatest contribution on the part of the parent should come before the child ever begins his formal education.*

If a parent will take the time to introduce his child to basic concepts which the parent, himself, uses all the time, think of the increase in his child's chances to succeed! Imagine a child's feeling of confidence when he finds he is already familiar with many of the things his kindergarten or first grade teacher is presenting to the class. How much more he can learn! How much better he feels about himself and about school!

There is a world of difference in the child whose parents are actively involved in his learning, and the child who is totally left on his own. It's a difference not only in ability, in quality of work, but also in attitude and self-image. Ask any teacher, any educator. You CAN make a difference.

Setting an Example: Like Parent, Like Child

While working in the yard one day, I came across a particularly large earthworm. I pointed it out to the 3-year-old who was tagging along behind me. "Ooh! Look at this nice big worm!" I exclaimed. The little girl squatted down for a closer look, unsure of what to think.

A few minutes later her mother appeared. "Look at the worm," pointed out the child.

"Ugh!" the mother grimaced.

"Yuck!" mimicked the daughter.

I sighed inside. While I'm not crazy about worms myself, I look at them without disgust or fear, and experience instead, a certain fascination that comes from observing other living things going about their business.

What happened in this particular situation was that the little girl was taught a lesson: earthworms are yucky and perhaps a little frightening. Without even realizing that she was communicating anything to her child, the mother expressed an emotional reaction for her to see. Because she is such a trusted person in her child's life, the mother's reactions have a special significance to the child.

Every parent has observed his child carefully study and copy a certain stance, or heard the child repeat, word for word, phrases (complete with identical inflection of the voice) he has heard you use.

Be aware, then, of your own tremendous power to affect your child's attitudes. Try to be conscious of the example you set, the message you pass on to your all-observing child. Where possible, avoid presenting reactions which will teach a child to fear things he really has no reason to fear.

In the same way, by offering encouragement to those around you, by using kind words and presenting a positive and thoughtful attitude, you set a good example for your child to follow.

How to REALLY Listen

In the May 1982 issue of *Redbook* magazine, Connie Broughton wrote about a startling discovery she made after repeatedly going through the following routine with her 5-year-old.

When Connie was washing dishes, reading, or in some way occupied, her daughter, Kenzie, would come in and say, "Mama."

"Yes, Kenzie," Connie would answer gently, continuing her task.

Ten seconds of silence.

"Mama."

"Yes, Kenzie," Connie answers, still gently.

Ten more seconds of silence.

"Mama."

"What?" Connie answers, less gently.

Ten more second of silence.

"Ma-a-a-ma!" she yells.

"What do you want?" Connie yells back, not gently at all.

Then Kenzie would say, "I have two blue dresses," or "I saw a bird in the back yard." Such simple news should not have created such an angry situation. Connie knew this and felt guilty.

Finally one day Kenzie started again with "Mama," and Connie answered, "I'm listening!" Kenzie's reply was, "But you're not looking at me." As was so often the case, Connie *wasn't* looking at her daughter. She was listening, but not looking. As Connie looked, Kenzie said something. Connie answered, and her daughter went away happy.

Such a simple solution! How often do we hear or say, "Look at me when I'm talking to you!" Eye contact is what "tells" us another person is listening or paying attention to us. And yet Connie was not always looking her child in the eye when she spoke to her. Eye contact is part of common courtesy we should extend to *everyone*.

When Connie made a conscious effort to make eye contact with Kenzie, she noticed a dramatic improvement. The "Mama-What" routine was almost eliminated.

I wanted to repeat this story to you because I feel it presents an extremely useful idea for us as parents and teachers to think about. If you don't already, make an effort to *look* at your child when he talks to you or you to him. It's an easy change to make, and a worthwhile one.

How a Child Learns

THE STAGES OF LEARNING

Take two balls of clay, exactly the same size, and show them to a 3-year-old, and he will agree that they are alike, the same. Now take one and roll it into a sausage shape while the child watches. Set it in front of him alongside the remaining ball of clay, and ask him if they are still the same. "No," he will answer. "This one has more clay," he says, pointing to the sausage. You ask him why, and he responds, matter-of-factly, "It's longer."

Illogical as it appears to an adult, such is the logic of a typical 3-year-old. Swiss psychologist, Jean Piaget, pioneered the field of study which deals with the development of a child's intellect. He began with close observation of his own children, and then followed the development of many others. He watched, recorded, and categorized. He questioned those old enough to talk, about how they arrived at a certain answer.

Piaget discovered that there are distinct stages of development in a child's thinking, and that in each stage, there are characteristic ways of thinking. The *sensorimotor period*, which lasts from birth to 1½–2 years, includes the stage where, if an object is hidden, it no longer exists. Toward the end of the first year, the toddler begins to realize that just because an object can't be seen, it doesn't mean it's no longer there. The child's actions gradually become less haphazard and more purposeful. When he begins to put words together with objects and grasp the concept of *representation*, he is ready to pass into the second period.

The *preoperational period* follows the sensorimotor period and lasts up until 6½–7 years of age. (Keep in mind that the passage from one stage to another is not sudden or clearcut. A child may, for several months, exhibit actions and reasoning from two different periods.) This second stage is one in which the child judges entirely by appearance, as in the clay experiment described above.

Another well-known example of this stage of thinking is the experiment where a child is shown two identical glasses containing the exact same amount of juice. When the juice from one glass is poured into a shallow dish, however, the child sees the remaining glass as holding more juice than the dish. He cannot understand how quantity can be the same when appearance has changed so drastically! The concept which the child cannot yet grasp is called *conservation of quantity*. Experiments also revealed similar reactions to apparent changes in length and number.

Piaget believed that until a child develops the *concept of reversibility*, the idea that the juice can be poured back into the glass, or the clay molded back into a ball, he cannot understand the concepts of conservation. He must first be able to visualize the reversals.

During this preoperational period, the child also thinks a person on the other side of the room sees things exactly as he does. He is aware only of his own point of view. He also has a difficult time considering a whole and its parts at the same time. When a pile of buttons is divided into blue buttons and red, the child sees only the two new sets of buttons. The group of buttons as a whole no longer exists.

At about the age of 7, a child enters the period of *concrete operations*. A child who has reached this third period understands the concepts of conservation and the relationship between a whole and its parts. His thinking seems fairly logical to adults, but he has a difficult time dealing with abstract ideas.

The child enters the fourth period at about 11 years of age. This period, which lasts until the child is 14 or 15, is called the period of *formal operations*. During these years, the child learns to see beyond reality, to consider more than the concrete. He can visualize the potential of things and deal with ideas. His development and experiences during this period lead him to adult reasoning.

The question we, as parents and teachers, ask is, "Can the transition from one stage to the next be accelerated?"

While there are those who feel we have no more control over the rate of a child's intellectual development than we do over when his teeth come in, Piaget felt and others feel we definitely do. *Piaget believed that although the order in which the thinking skills are learned is fixed, the rate is not.* A stimulating environment can affect the child's development. He strongly opposed high-pressure acceleration from one stage to the next.

Even more than Piaget, American psychologist, Jerome Bruner, sees the enrichment of a child's environment as opening up enormous possibilities concerning his intellectual development. Bruner believes that humans have three systems for processing information: action, visual images, and (the most sophisticated) symbols. While adults are able to switch from one system to another, children depend on the first two. Bruner's own experiments revealed most success when combining manipulation and labeling.

Both Piaget and Bruner expressed the belief that the most valuable contribution a parent or teacher can make to a child is to provide numerous and varied opportunities for discovery through use of manipulative materials. *To grasp a real understanding of the world around him, a child must observe, handle, play with, and experiment with the many things in his environment.*

HEMISPHERIC SPECIALIZATION

When I stop to consider it, it is incomprehensible to me that my brain and body can function with such coordination and with virtually no conscious effort on my part. I am astounded by the fact that my fingers can so easily maneuver a pencil to put on paper the words my mind is thinking. To think that the messages which stimulate the right side of my body originate in the left hemisphere of my brain is fascinating!

In recent years, more and more research has been done on the brain and its two sides, or hemispheres, which, while they appear symmetrical, seem to have definite structural and functional differences. There is a distinct set of skills associated with each of the two hemispheres.

The left hemisphere is said to be in use for skills such as handwriting, reading, language, phonics, following directions, and listening. The right hemisphere is involved in spatial relationships, math computation, singing and music, creativity, feelings and emotions, and art expression.

While left-hemispheric people think in symbols, deal in symbols, and can function with symbols, right hemispheric people deal with the concrete, learn by doing, touching, moving, being in the middle of things.

Although we all use both hemispheres, we tend to use one side more than the other. It is in this dominant hemisphere that we process information first. If we can learn to balance the strength of our two hemispheres, we can come closer to achieving our potential.

Problems can arise when a child who is right hemisphere-dominant enters school and must deal with what is primarily a "left-brained curriculum." Rather than fault the child, we must question our teaching methods and learn to find alternatives to meet each child's individual needs. While left-hemispheric people deal in and learn through symbols, right-brained people learn more by doing, touching and moving. It's not hard to imagine how difficult it might be for a right-brained child to learn most academic skills.

How do you determine if your child is right-brained? Simple observation can help. Many, but not all right-brained children have difficulty following directions, use a lot of gestures with their speech, have trouble with phonics, and like to take things apart and put them back together.

Another thing to consider is the fact that while right-handers may be left or right-brained, left-handers are almost always right-brained.

If you think your child may be right-brained, I would suggest doing some research into the subject and putting extra effort into adjusting activities to better suit his learning style. Even if your child appears to be left-brained, stimulating his right hemisphere is valuable as it can help him learn to process information in different ways and develop the less dominant hemisphere of his brain. Below are some activities which involve the use of the right hemisphere of the brain. Also, see chapter 10: "Creative Thinking" which includes right-brained activities.

Activities for the Right Side of the Brain

➡ Consider playing music while your child is working on a skill. It may help a right-brained child focus his attention longer and think better.

➡ Incorporate physical movement into learning activities whenever possible. For example, combine a set of dancing steps with counting or spelling or reciting the alphabet.

➡ Perform a simple series of movements (touch your toes, turn around and clap your hands) and ask your child to repeat it. Try another series of movements and ask him to *tell* what you did.

➡ Make use of a chalkboard often to draw diagrams, maps or simple illustrations to accompany descriptions and explanations of things. (Ideally, all teaching should include both verbal and visual cues.)

➡ Develop a special language using simple pictures (rather than words) that you can use to leave messages for your child and vice versa.

➡ With a child who is learning letters and numbers, make a game of writing them on his back. Ask him to name the letter or number he felt. Trade places and let your child write on your back! You could also use this technique to identify geometric shapes.

➡ Encourage drawing and painting. These activities require a strong shift to the right hemisphere.

➡ When introducing a new word in response to your child's "What is that?", go beyond providing the label, the word for the object. Help your child learn as many of the characteristics of the object as possible. For example, when introducing the word "apple," let your child feel a real apple. Talk about it's shape, color and texture. With a child who already knows the word "apple," there are lots of things to do with an apple! Cut the apple open and look inside. Point out the seeds and explain their purpose. When you've talked about how apples grow, and what we can do with them, let your child eat it. Help him see that an apple is so much more than the word "apple."

Tools of the Trade

As in any job, it is much easier to teach if you have a set of guidelines and all the needed tools. Below are some basic "rules" to keep in mind when working with your child, and a list of materials to help you in your role of teacher.

✔ Learning is not limited to a school-like setting. Learning can take place in the yard, the bathtub, the car, the grocery store—virtually anywhere! The parent's job is to ask, "What can I help my child experience and learn from this?"

✔ If your child shows no interest in an activity, STOP! He's not ready for it. When he is, he will learn more quickly and easily. *Pressuring a child will do more harm than good.*

✔ Stop an activity *before* your child wants to, before he has had a chance to get tired of it. This way the fun remains and learning is a treat.

✔ Don't play learning games with a child who has just misbehaved. You don't want him to connect the activity with punishment. He should learn that such games are only for a child who behaves.

✔ Before you say "No" to an activity, ask yourself if it's really going to hurt anything if your child gets muddy, or bangs the spoon on cans and chairs, or turns his tricycle over to watch the wheels spin. After taking safety into account, let your child try things, investigate, question. That's how he learns about the world around him.

✔ Join your child in some spontaneous silliness. This gives your child "permission" to try new things without fear of ridicule.

✔ Provide your child with as many first-hand experiences as possible. Going to a zoo is far more valuable than reading about animals in a book or seeing them on television. Active learning is always more valuable than passive learning.

✔ When your child asks you to show him how to tie his shoes for the 50th time, or make the letter "S" five days in a row, hold on to the sigh of exasperation, look at that face, and begin AGAIN. Remind yourself that learning takes time. If you're lucky, you'll be there when the spark ignites, the face lights up, and at last, you hear a confident, "Oh, I get it!"

✔ Remember that it is better to work with your child for short periods of time (15 minutes or less), more often than for longer periods of time, less often.

✔ When a child runs into a problem, don't rush to solve it for him. Allow him to express some frustration, and encourage him to figure out a solution. For example, if your child has trouble pulling his wagon up stairs because the wheels get caught, wait a few moments before calmly suggesting that he try pulling up on the handle more. Your verbal encouragement shows your child that you *recognize his dilemma and have confidence in his ability to get himself out of it.* If, after giving it a fair try, he still can't get the wagon up the steps, by all means, lend a hand.

✔ It is important that you let your child do things for himself whenever possible. It would certainly be faster for you to dress your child each morning, but if he's going to learn to dress himself, you're going to have to let him try! If it's too hard to watch, go into another room and offer help only if he asks for it.

✔ One of the greatest gifts you can give your child is a positive attitude toward learning. If you and your child have fun together discovering and practicing new skills and ideas, your child will have no reason to consider learning as anything but an enjoyable experience. Your enthusiasm is the key.

✔ If, while you are playing a game with your child, he invents his own variation, go along with it. He may have made the change to better suit his own capabilities and interests. He may have been simply exercising his creativity. Be flexible—most of all, you want the activity to be enjoyable.

✔ Although spending time playing and talking with your child is essential, keep in mind that he also needs unscheduled, free time to play with neighborhood friends or be by himself.

 There are certain aids to teaching which definitely make the job easier. Below is a list of materials which will make home-teaching easier. You can use your imagination to find substitutes and extras.

✔ Table or desk.

✔ Chalkboard. For some reason, children love to write on a chalkboard. What better incentive to get your child to enjoy learning? (Mistakes erase easily. Success remains in mind.) The bigger the chalkboard, the better.

✔ Lots of paper: lined, unlined, and colorful construction paper.

✔ Soft lead pencils and erasers.

✔ Crayons, colored pencils, and felt-tipped markers.

✔ Wall map of the world and/or a globe or an atlas.

✔ Wall map of the U.S.

✔ Dictionary *at the appropriate level for your child.*

✔ Scissors and glue.

✔ Ruler.

✔ Old magazines for cutting and making collages.

✔ Set of encyclopedias. (Some are more appropriate for use by children than others.)

✔ Unlined index cards, and red and black magic markers for making flashcards.

✔ Water colors, tempera paints, and large paint brushes.

YOUR CHILD'S SELF-ESTEEM

A *child who feels good about himself, who has a good self-concept, learns more easily than does a child with low self-esteem.* In their book, *100 Ways to Enhance Self-Concept in the Classroom,* Jack Canfield and Harold Wells describe studies which support this statement. In most classrooms, it is all too evident that those children who have the most trouble academically usually have a low self-concept. ("I can't do it. I'm just too stupid!") The two seem to go hand in hand. Attempts to teach a child academics are less likely to succeed unless work in developing self-concept is done concurrently. At the same time, without a firm grasp of the 3 R's, a child has a hard time feeling good about himself, especially in the realm of school, and thus the beginning of that self-defeating cycle.

A child whose self-esteem is high, learns more easily because he enjoys the challenge of acquiring new skills and information. He approaches new experiences and new tasks with an "I can do it" attitude. An environment which respects a child as an individual, which communicates an understanding of his needs, and which surrounds him with a warm and nurturing love, provides him with the best chance of succeeding academically and developing into an emotionally healthy human being.

In order for the rest of this book to "do its job", you as a parent, must make a commitment to helping your child feel good about himself. If he knows you have confidence in his abilities to succeed, he will believe it, too, and then there's no limit to what he (and you, too) can accomplish!

The Importance of Love

What parent can look at his sleeping child and not feel an overwhelming rush of affection? One's parental love for that unique individual, that innocent-looking child who only hours before was perhaps the epitome of a "terrible two", is difficult to describe. It is something which is felt with one's heart.

How you express this love to your child tells him a great deal about himself. In order to consider himself lovable and therefore valued, your child must feel your love. You must make a conscious effort to show it with more than hugs and the words "I love you."

When you are doing something with your child, it is important that he feel you are with him mentally as well as physically. If you decide to take 15 minutes to read a book with your child, for instance, tell yourself you are going to forget the dishes, the office, the bills, etc. for these 15 minutes. Allow yourself to become completely involved in being with your child. Spend those 15 minutes really looking at and listening to your child. Letting him know that you enjoy being with him is the greatest boost you can give to his self-esteem. By choosing him over the television, or by asking him to help you wash the car or go fishing, you tell him that he is a worthwhile person, someone you like to be with.

When you pick your child up at the day-care center or when you get home from work, make a point of letting him know right away how glad you are to see him. This tells him that you missed him because he's important in your life.

Loving your child also means respecting him as a person. Treat him with the same courtesy you would a friend. Use "please" and "thank you", knock before entering his room, and if a reprimand is coming, wait until his friends or siblings have left before delivering it. Consider his feelings as you would anyone else's.

If your child feels you appreciate his uniqueness, he will feel free to express it. It is important that he doesn't feel the need to be a carbon copy of someone else. In his book, *Love*, Leo Buscaglia reminds the reader of an idea that all parents should help their children believe in: "You are the best you. You will always be the second best anyone else."

Finally, save some love for yourself. Don't expect to be a perfect parent—no one is. We can't feel blind love for our children 24 hours a day. We all become frustrated by our children at times, say things we later regret, and feel disappointed in ourselves for failing to control our emotions and tempers. Take advantage of these not-so-pleasant situations to later explain to your child that you were upset about his behavior, and that you needed to let off a little steam like he does sometimes, but that no matter what, you still love him. Your child will appreciate your honesty and the fact that you consider him deserving of an explanation. Rest assured that if your child feels you love him, and the majority of his interactions with you are positive, the few minor negative incidents that occur are not going to cause real damage.

Your Expectations

The fact that you are reading this book proves that you believe in your ability to influence your child's development. One of the most crucial tasks you face is setting expectations, because *your child measures his own adequacy according to how well he matches your expectations.* If they are too low, the child feels he must be incapable of achieving much, and that you don't have faith in his ability to accomplish and succeed. Equally harmful is holding expectations which are too high. The inevitable and repeated failures which result, serve only to create in the child, feelings of worthlessness.

The question then is, "How do I come up with realistic expectations?" In her book, *Your Child's Self-Esteem*, Dorothy Corkille Briggs explains several factors for a parent to consider in developing reasonable expectations. First, take into account facts on child development. You want to challenge your child but not ask for more than he can give. For example, to expect a 2-year-old to sit patiently in a waiting room while a car is being serviced, or go to bed "as usual" when visiting grandparents, is unfair. A parent with an understanding of the 2-year-old will take his child for a walk whenever waiting for any length of time is required, and allow for special treatment when the child is going to bed away from home. Briggs also feels that it is important to observe one's own child closely and take into account his individual likes and dislikes, his behavior in different situations. Before coming up with expectations, watch your child and learn to know his way of handling experiences.

Realistic expectations also take into consideration the child's past and present pressures. Remember that a child's behavior is usually affected to some degree by a stressful situation such as the birth of a sibling, the death of a grandparent, or moving to a new home.

I strongly feel that most parents could raise their expectations for their children and do no damage, for the simple reason that I think children during the first six years of life are capable of and enjoy learning far more than most parents realize. As long as they're reasonable, more challenges mean more successes and a stronger feeling of "I can do it!"

At the same time, there is nothing anywhere that says once you've made an expectation, you can't lower it. If your child has trouble handling or succeeding at something you've introduced him to, lower your expectation, and change the goal to one which is attainable. Be flexible! Who cares if he's not ready to ride his bike without training wheels at the age his older brother was? Rather than have him fall repeatedly, put the training wheels back on, go for a bike ride with him, and let him know that you're glad to be with him whether he's using training wheels or not. If you spend time making a learning game and your child doesn't show any interest in it, then he obviously isn't ready for the concept. Don't show your disappointment. Put the game away until a later date. He'll be ready for it eventually, and then watch the smiles as he learns something new. It will be worth the wait.

Let Your Child Be a Child

Sue and I played with dolls until we were probably 12, and my junior high years were pretty much devoted to my horse. My long-standing "boyfriend" was the one I danced with at dancing class and wrote about in my diary. Most girls I knew didn't really start dating until they were 15 or 16 years old. Television meant shows like "Bonanza," "Father Knows Best," and "My Three Sons"— very "moral", family-type entertainment.

Let's face it. Things aren't quite the same today. Ours is a nation that rushes on highways to supermarkets, one-hour film processing stores, and fast food restaurants. We invent innumerable household gadgets to save time, and build leisure craft to go faster than ever. Children enter serious athletic competition at incredibly early ages, and we dress them in miniature versions of adult clothes.

In his book entitled *The Hurried Child*, David Elkind describes some of the more negative results of hurrying children, problems which show up in adolescence: an increase in the number of headaches and stomachaches in children that appear to be stress-related; an increase in teenage suicides; a rise in the number of cults; a rise in teenage crime; and a rush to experiment sexually (and the increase in venereal disease in teens).

There are, Elkind feels, a number of things at the root of the problem: parents today are generally under more stress than they were 20 years ago; more parents are alone because of divorce or separation; an increase in crime has caused more fear in general; and parents are more professionally insecure due to threats of technology and inflation. As a result, parents find a need to be more absorbed with themselves. Unfortunately, good child-rearing requires distancing from one's own needs.

Elkind describes the pressures put on children by schools, and the influence of television which has undergone dramatic changes over the years. He also reminds the reader that a child simply does not think, learn, or feel in the same way that an adult does. We need to be careful how much we ask of a child and be sure that our demands are appropriate for his age. We're not being fair if we ask him to grow up too fast.

I worry that we, as parents, as teachers, and as a society, do not stop often enough and say, "Boy, are you lucky to be young!" Too often we allow our children to be treated as adults. At times, we may even encourage adult behaviors because it seems easier—at least at the moment. We need to stop and remind ourselves that this person is still a child. He can't make decisions as to how much of an adult he should be. All he knows is the pressure around him to be a small grown-up. It's our job as adults to set the limits, to tell our children when it's appropriate to be more grown up, and when it's not.

We need to remind our children that they are still children, and help them feel OK about behaving like children! I'm sure that at times that's exactly what most children need (and want) to hear.

Comparing Children

To be sure each child feels that he is an individual, a special person, be careful not to compare your children. Many parents assume that a good parent treats all his or her children the same. On the contrary, children don't like being treated the same. They prefer to be treated differently, as unique individuals.

When John does something new for him, and you say, "Oh, I remember when Susie did that," you tell John that what he did has already been done by his older sister who does things so much better than he can anyway. That may not be what you meant, but that is what he understands.

Be prepared for your children to perform and progress differently in school. While you want them to do well, it's not uncommon for one child to excel in math and the other in reading. One may be strong academically, and the other athletically. Encourage and help a child to improve in those areas in which he is weak, but also let him know how proud you are of his strengths.

Allow each child his own bedtime and nighttime routine. Read each one a different story, allowing him time alone with you. Let an older child stay up later, even if only by 15 minutes. Recognize each as an individual.

Mistakes—An Important Part of Learning

No matter how fair and reasonable your expectations, your child is going to make mistakes as he is learning. They are part of the process; they go with the territory. One of your roles as a parent is to talk with your child about mistakes and not reaching one's goal, about doing something "wrong." We all fail to get the right answer sometimes, to say the right thing, to win a ball game, or to write a clear sentence.

Explain to your child that mistakes actually help us learn. We learn by reflecting on the feedback we receive. If that feedback tells us that we've done something incorrectly, then it's up to us to do something about it, to correct the mistake. Most importantly, you want your child to be willing to try again or try a different approach—one that might work better for him—in order to achieve the desired result. *Flexibility* is a very important learning tool.

Your child must be reminded consistently that *mistakes are part of learning.* If you make no mistakes, because something is too easy, then you are not dealing with anything new, and you're simply wasting your time. It's actually important for your child to make mistakes—not a lot, but yes, once in a while, so that he knows what it is like to miss the mark, and how to come back and try again. The possibility of making errors is something we must all deal with constantly, and it will be less painful or devastating if the situation is not completely new.

You want your child to be comfortable trying new things. Help him see that only by risking failure does he also stand a chance of succeeding, gaining, learning something new. Encourage curiosity, experimentation and risk-taking. They are valuable and worthwhile qualities to nurture.

Be sure your child knows that while you expect him always to do his best, you also realize he's not perfect. No one is. There is no reason to pretend that we as adults are perfect and infallible. Children learn a great deal from seeing us recognize our imperfections, admit our mistakes, and work on correcting them.

Warm Fuzzies: Let's Be Positive!

I was blindfolded and my hands tied behind me. Slowly but deliberately, my captors led me, one at each arm, along the hall, down the stairs, and into a room where at last the journey ended. My blindfold was removed and suddenly I heard shouts.

"Surprise!" From behind tables and under desks, my students appeared. Balloons, which had been hung around the room, suddenly popped, as my hands were untied, and I was led to stand before a cake. On it were written the words, "We'll miss you, Mrs. Jones." Around the message were the names of the students.

Needless to say, a large lump suddenly developed in my throat. I was touched by the thoughtfulness and effort which had gone into this special event. "What a terrific warm fuzzy!" I told my students.

Warm fuzzies are all those things we can say or do for others to encourage them, and boost their feelings of self-esteem. In learning to give warm fuzzies, a child begins to consider the feelings of others, to emphathize.

The day following the surprise party described above, I talked seriously with my class. It was the last day of school, and there were some things I wanted to say. One was how proud I was of their growth in thoughtfulness and being positive with one another.

Gym class had been the primary target of my year-long preaching. I had asked repeatedly that they all try to encourage each other and help those students who were less certain of themselves on the playing field. We talked about when and why people feel unsure of themselves. We discussed how to best help people feel better about trying, getting involved in a game.

We talked many times about how it feels when someone puts you down for making a mistake, and the fact that putting someone down only makes it less likely that that person will want to try any more.

I tried to help my students realize that only by encouraging reluctant players to join in, will those players become more skillful, and thus better team members. This last was for a long time a major concern of those who were already skilled. A child who grew more confident as a result of being included in a game and encouraged to be a part of the team, learned not only to play better, but to feel better about himself. This, I pointed out, was the most important goal of all.

During gym class, I shouted, "Good kick!" and "Nice try!" from the sidelines, and reminded everyone that I wanted to hear lots of warm fuzzies and encouragement. Eventually the words became more automatic. Children who had been watchers became participants. At the end of the year, I let the class vote on a number of awards, one of which was "Most Improved Athlete." The boy who won was stunned but obviously pleased. His increase in assertiveness and improved skills had been justly recognized by the rest of the class.

That last day of school, when I told my students how proud I was of them, I was rewarded in turn by the student who said, "You know who taught us that? You did!"

It is indeed possible to teach children to be positive, encouraging, and more thoughtful human beings. Change takes time and constant attention, but eventually it brings its own reward. Better yet, set good examples in these areas of values and your child will grow up exhibiting the same positive attitude about himself and toward others.

Remember When . . .?

Can you remember what it was like to be a child, how you felt in certain situations, what made you feel secure and what left you feeling very small, alone, and afraid?

Most of us don't reflect much on our childhood. This is natural, as the majority of our experiences of youth don't often seem relevant to our roles as adults. And yet, perhaps they should, for if we are parents and teachers, how can we really relate to and understand our children if we always remain "the adult"?

I don't mean to say that we should try to be our children's pals and join in all their activities, but we should watch, listen, and recall the feelings we see our children experiencing. Keep in mind that it's not easy for a child to feel comfortable talking to someone whose physical size reminds him how small and powerless he is. When talking to children, we should literally bring ourselves to their level and squat down, kneel, or sit on the floor.

Children seem to have a cruel knack for making fun of each other, laughing at others' frailties and finding sensitive spots. ("You're so skinny!" "What a haircut! You're practically bald!") As adults, we have, for the most part, learned to "consider the source" and to handle the insensitivities of others. We have better things to do with our time than getting upset over thoughtless words, or so we tell ourselves.

Yet, to a child, such experiences can be earth-shattering. To be singled out as different, to be humiliated at an age when one's identity is still developing, is a frightening and lonely thing. When your child experiences something "devastating", imagine yourself in his place. Think back to those days when your ideals and values were much the same as his are now. Relate to your child an experience you had once that made you want to run and hide or cry. He will probably be amazed and also quite relieved to know that you, too, once felt that way.

A child who is hurting inside doesn't need to be smothered with affection and told it doesn't matter. To the child, it does matter! A parent's role becomes one of supporting and explaining. Listen with empathy (use your heart, not your head), and reflect back to the child what you hear him saying. "It sounds like you were really angry when she said that." This way you *offer understanding but not judgment.* If your child can trust you to accept his feelings, he can express them without fear of lecture or disapproval. Simply expressing his emotions will go a long way in ridding the child of destructive or emotionally-charged energy.

After listening to your child, offer hugs and security, but also deal with the problem. Discuss why the other children did what they did, and ask your child what he sees as his alternatives for dealing with the situation. Help him to deal with the present and develop a reasonable set of responses for the next time such a situation occurs.

Keep in mind that young as they are, children appreciate certain characteristics in adults. They want and need consistency, as in rules and consequences. Children don't like to be nagged or criticized in front of others any more than adults do. They are extremely sensitive to honesty and dishonesty, and are usually more than willing to accept an apology or an admission of "I don't know" when it is offered sincerely.

Whenever a situation arises that your child is physically too small to handle, rather than comment on his "shortcoming" ("You're too short to reach that shelf"), make it a problem with the object ("That shelf is too high. Let me help").

It takes real effort to start looking at things the way a child does, but it can also be an intriguing challenge. Fred Rogers, on his program, *Mr. Rogers' Neighborhood*, does it better than anyone I've seen. Make a point of watching his show sometime to see how he introduces new ideas and experiences. He demonstrates a very definite understanding of how a child thinks, and the questions a child would ask in each situation. He also anticipates the emotional reactions a child might have and accepts them without judgment.

The Role of Literature in Developing Self-Awareness

Every child deals with a lot of feelings and situations about which he has questions. By reading and discussing stories with your child, you can provide him with a means of exploring emotions and how to deal with them.

Literature can help a child recognize his feelings and be aware of things that children do and don't do to cope with these feelings. A child is more apt to accept himself if, through stories, he sees other children with similar problems, worries, or conflicts. The great value in literature is that discussing a character in a story is a safe and impersonal way of looking at a problem; it is a nonaccusing, nonlecturing and nonjudgmental setting, because the child himself is not personally involved.

In reading a book with your child, your role becomes that of thought provoker. You want to discuss in a comfortable, speculative manner, what the character was feeling at a certain time, what motivated him to do what he did, what he might have done differently, how the choices he made might affect him in the long run, and so on.

One of our main tasks as parent or educator is to help a child recognize his emotions and find acceptable outlets for those emotions. If you don't already do so, please consider reading to your child at bedtime. Besides providing an opportunity to discuss different topics, feelings, and ideas, reading books with a child can remind us of what a child's world is like. Children's books can put us in touch with what is and what isn't important to a child.

The following is a list of books which have been written for preschool and primary-grade children about dealing with specific problems. These and more can be found in libraries and bookstores.

SEPARATION
Dear Phoebe *by Sue Alexander*
Be Good Harry *by Mary Chalmers*
Will I Have a Friend? *by Miriam Cohen*
You Go Away *by Dorothy Corey*
Lost and Found *by Kathryn Hitte*
Going to Day Care *by Fred (Mister) Rogers*
Daddy and Ben Together *by Miriam Stecher and Alice Kandell*

SIBLING RELATIONSHIPS
Dumb Stupid David *by Dorothy Aldis*
Amy and the New Baby *by Myra Berry Brown*
The New Baby At Your House *by Joanna Cole*
The New Baby *by Fred Rogers*
This Room is Mine *by Betty Wright*
The Quarreling Book *by Charlotte Zolotov*
War With Grandpa *by Robert K. Smith*

DIVORCE
Where is Daddy? The Story of A Divorce *by Beth Goff*
Emily and the Klunky Baby and the Next-door Dog *by Joan Lexau*
Divorce is a Grown-Up Problem *by Janet Sinberg*

HANDICAPS
Howie Helps Himself *by Joan Fassler*
One Little Girl *by Joan Fassler*
I Have a Sister, My Sister is Deaf *by Jean Whitehouse*

DEATH
The Dead Bird *by Margaret Wise Brown*
My Grandpa Died Today *by Joan Fassler*
The Tenth Good Thing About Barney *by Judith Viorst*

ADOPTION
The Really Real Family *by Helen Doss*
Abby *by Jeannette Caines*
I Am Adopted *by Susan Lapsley*

OTHER
Don't Worry, Dear *by Joan Fassler*

Activities to Help Your Child Develop a Positive Self-Concept

 ➡ At the end of the day, at the dinner table or at bedtime, have your child share the successes he experienced that day. You may have to help at first. Point out the things he accomplished, and help him see that he does indeed accomplish, learn, and succeed every day.

➡ Choose a quiet place to play a sentence completion game. Take time to share the thoughts and feelings behind the answers given.

If I could have one wish, it would be . . .
I am happiest when . . .
I get angry when . . .
People think I am . . .
I think I am . . .
I don't like people who . . .
Something I do well is . . .
Something I'm getting better at is . . .
I don't like people to help me with . . .

➡ Talk about *warm fuzzies* and *cold pricklies.* Warm fuzzies are things done or said to make a person feel good about himself. ("Hey, I can see you worked hard on this." "Good try! You'll get it next time." "I sure appreciate your help.") Cold pricklies are things said or done which make a person feel less than good about himself. ("Can't you do that?" "Boy, are you dumb." "I can't believe you struck out!") Set aside a special time each week to give warm fuzzies to each other as a family.

➡ Make a Warm Fuzzy Poster. Anyone who catches another member of the family doing something good, writes about it on the poster and signs his name. (A non-writer could ask an older family member to write for him.) Make a point of reading each addition to the list at a time when the family is together. (Examples would be: "I saw Jenny help Mom vaccuum. Pat.", "I watched Paul get his shirt on all by himself. Mark.")

CHAPTER

3

DEVELOPING SKILLS FOR LEARNING

Listening Skills and Following Directions

A mother looks at her five-year-old son who is sitting at the kitchen table, painting a picture. "John," she asks, "would you please go get the dirty laundry from your room?"

"Mmhmm," he answers, not moving from his chair.

After a minute, the mother realizes that her son still hasn't moved. "I guess you don't have any," she comments.

John looks up long enough to ask, "Any what?"

"Laundry," she reminds him. "I asked you to get your dirty clothes so I can wash them."

"You did?" he responds. "OK," and he heads for his room and the pile of muddy clothes his mother knows is there.

Not long afterward, the washing machine is sloshing and John is at the table, working on his painting. His mother watches him for a moment.

"I don't suppose you'd like some ice cream," she says.

"Sure," the boy answers, standing up immediately, his artwork quickly forgotten.

Funny how John heard "ice cream" so much more easily than he had heard "laundry", even over the noise of the washing machine! And yet, not really so funny. John's mother begins to wonder how often her son "tunes her out."

As a teacher in the classroom, I worry about the number of learning opportunities that are missed by students simply because they are not listening. By the time a child reaches high school and college, 75 percent of his academic learning will be through listening, the rest through reading. So the sooner he learns to really listen, the better.

With a young child, it is important to remember that his attention span is short and his vocabulary limited. If you continue a discussion for too long or use too many words he doesn't yet understand, he will learn to tune you out. At first, don't expect a child to listen for more than a few minutes to your explanations of how something works or descriptions of things. As he comes to see that your words offer interesting information, he will listen for longer periods of time.

You can best train your child to listen and follow directions by beginning a request with his name. When you're sure you have his attention, give the directions once and only once. They might be, "Peter, I'd like you to put your book away and set the table please." If he's busy and ignores you, go to him and calmly ask him, "Do you remember what I asked you to do a few minutes ago?" If he admits he wasn't listening, explain in a serious tone of voice that you expect him to do as he's asked the first time. Be sure to praise him when he does follow your directions promptly. Be excited when your child shows he's learning to really listen. Your positive reinforcement will go much farther in teaching him to listen and respond than any negative consequences you come up with for his failure to do so.

Listening vs. Hearing: Is There a Problem?

One day while visiting a friend, I peeked into her 6-year-old son's room where he and my son were playing with cars.

"Wow, Seth, that's a nice truck," I commented. "Is it new?"

"What?" he asked with only a brief glance in my direction.

"Is that truck new?" I repeated.

Seth looked at me with a frown on his forehead, and said in a somewhat exasperated voice, "I don't know!"

Rather than embarrass Seth again by repeating my question, I walked back to my friend in the kitchen, feeling somewhat confused. Seth's "I don't know" had been so inappropriate that I had to wonder if he'd heard me correctly. His mother described how she and her husband felt frustrated at times by their son's failure to listen to them, to respond to simple requests.

Not long after the incident described above, a trip to the doctor for an ear infection revealed that Seth not only had an ear infection, but that he was suffering from a severe loss of hearing. When antibiotics failed to clear up the problem, tubes were put in his ears. Within two weeks, his hearing had improved dramatically.

Needless to say, Seth's parents felt terribly guilty about having gotten upset with him for not following directions when in fact, he hadn't heard them! They wondered, too, when the hearing loss had occurred, and how much Seth had missed of what was going on in his first grade class before the problem was detected.

The reason for including this story is obvious. If you have any reason to suspect your child might have a problem with his hearing, have it tested by a physician right away.

Listening Activities

❶ Listening skills can be improved by simply reading to your child *regularly.*

❷ Ask your child questions about the stories you read to him. Encourage him to tell you what the story was about and remember important details. If this process proves too difficult, discuss the story a page at a time, gradually lengthening the number of pages covered.

❸ Once in a while, sit somewhere with your child, close your eyes, and see how many different sounds you can identify. Or, take a walk with your child and have him keep a record of the different sounds he hears and how often each occurs. (Examples: dog barks, screeching brakes, voices, sirens, leaves rustling, birds chirping or singing.) Your child may want to draw a picture of these sounds when the walk is over.

4 Listen to and memorize songs, and sing them together in the car, while you're cooking, or weeding the garden.

5 Clap a rhythm pattern or tap it with a pencil and ask your child to repeat it. Start simple and add varied rhythms as your child's skill develops.

6 Give your child a series of oral directions to follow such as "Walk to the door, turn around in a circle, and hop back to the couch." Work up to as many actions as your child can handle without getting frustrated. This is a good activity for developing motor skills as well as listening skills.

7 Hide an object in a room and clap to provide clues to help him locate the object. Clap loudly as he moves toward it, and softly as he moves away. This is great fun played with several children clapping while one hunts.

8 Read numbers for your child to repeat in order. Start with two-number sequences and increase as your child is ready.

9 Say short sentences and ask your child to repeat them to you. Take turns building longer add-a-word sentences when your child can repeat the shorter ones without too much difficulty. (Example: The girl swam. The little girl swam. The little girl swam in the pool.) These can be very funny, and are fun for the whole family to build together on car trips or at the beach.

10 Say a word and have your child share a word that rhymes with it.

11 Say two words that are either exactly the same or slightly different, and have your child tell you if they're the same or different. (Example: hit and hat; bed and bad)

12 You can play a game where you say three words, two of which begin with the same sound. Ask your child to tell you which word begins with a different sound than the other two. (Example: monkey, lemon, man)

13 Here's an old one that is still going strong, and an excellent skill builder. Pretend you're going on a trip and each person adds a new object to the list of things being taken. For example, the first person might say, "I'm going on a trip and I'm taking a toothbrush." The second person would repeat the first sentence and add to it. "I'm going on a trip and I'm taking a toothbrush and a book." And so on.

14 Play Simple Simon.

Developing Responsibility

Some children, when they begin school, are already responsible. Their teachers seldom have to ask them twice to do something. These children do their chores and schoolwork without being nagged. They accept the work as something that needs to be done, so they do it. Lucky are these children, for their lives will be much more pleasant as a result of having learned to be responsible.

Too many children, however, procrastinate, argue, complain, avoid, and simply don't do those things for which they are responsible. How does a parent deal with a child who shows patterns of irresponsible behavior? Is there really hope? Most definitely, yes—if you are willing to work at it. There is some time, interest, and effort required on your part, but you will be doing your child a great service if you will help him in this matter.

In any situation where your child has trouble doing as you've asked, you can instill responsible behavior by setting up rules along the pattern of: "When you have _____, then you may _____," or "Before you can _____, you must _____." You don't have to set up special rewards or incentives, either. Simply choose an activity your child likes to do and takes for granted, such as riding his bike, having friends over, or going outside to play. Then you require that he complete a less desirable act first. In other words, require that he take a bath (put away his toys, or empty the trash) before he can play with his friends (or watch television). This doesn't have to be done in a punishing or even disciplinary manner. Rather, it usually works best if said matter-of-factly, with the message that this is the way life is—we meet our responsibilities and then we play.

Perhaps one of the most effective ways of helping your child become more responsible is to choose a behavior which shows his lack of responsibility and work to change it. It needs to be something you can measure in some way. For instance, how many times he is late to dinner, how many times he makes his bed without being reminded (not often enough!), or how often he puts his dirty clothes in the laundry.

After you've decided on a behavior you want to change, you need to find an incentive the child is willing to work for. Talk it over with him. You might make a chart and place stars, stickers, or points on it each time he shows the behavior you want. You should probably have a long-term goal and reward for your child to work toward—a friend over for the night, or a picnic and swimming. After all, changing behavior is difficult for all of us, at any age, and recognition makes us proud of our accomplishments. Children and parents are no different in this respect.

Once your reward system has been set up, your child is on his own to remember his chore, with no reminder from you. No star or sticker unless the behavior was accomplished exactly as agreed upon. (Don't require stickers to be earned each day of the week, or a child who goofs on Monday will give up the rest of the week.)

Be sure to let your child know how proud of him you are each time he remembers on his own. *Make it pleasant and worthwhile for him to be responsible.* It can be done. There will be some backsliding, but learning to be responsible is a lesson worth pursuing. It will pay off in every area of your child's development, and will go a long way in helping him to make a smooth adjustment to school.

TRUST

Tied in closely with responsibility is trust. It is important for you to create situations in which you place trust in your child. For example, let him in on a secret. It can be as simple as, "We're having ice cream sundaes for dessert, but don't tell your father or your sister. It's our secret!" You can also help your child feel proud, trusted, and responsible by allowing him to carry the ice cream sundaes to the table.

If you've got the television turned to the evening news and you are listening while you're busy with something else, you might ask your child to remind you when the weather comes on. You're giving him the responsibility of watching for the weather report and alerting you. He'll like the chance to feel important and helpful.

You might consider getting your child a small pet to care for, something along the lines of a goldfish or a hamster. Or, you might give him a plant for his room. Being trusted to care for a living thing can often be a great incentive to behave responsibly.

As with anything, responsibility will not be learned overnight. The plant may die, the secret of the ice cream spilled, or the reminder about the weather forgotten, but these mistakes only mean that your child needs more practice and more encouragement to become a more responsible person. Avoid showing great disappointment or you'll snuff out the enthusiasm to even try things. If a child thinks he's going to be scolded for making mistakes, he's not going to want to place himself in the position of trying something new or difficult.

DEVELOPING A LOVE OF READING

The Good Old-Fashioned Bedtime Story

One day, after lunch, I had nearly half my class in tears. It was the girls who cried, while the boys remained silent, their faces intent, their eyes wide.

I found myself struggling to maintain composure as I sat with my class that day, reading the final chapters of Wilson Rawls' *Where the Red Fern Grows.* I literally had to stop a few times to take a deep breath before I could continue.

Despite the huge lump in my throat, I was excited and satisfied to know how deeply words could affect my students. On numerous other occasions, while reading books like Roald Dahl's *The BFG,* my entire class would explode with laughter. My eyes would water from laughing so hard. There aren't many situations which are more wonderful than those times of shared tears or laughter. They create a warm sense of closeness between the reader and anyone listening to the story.

Not only do words have the ability to evoke emotions, to stir the reader to laugh or cry, but they also have the power to generate thoughts and questions, to start a reader's brain wondering, imagining.

The repeated incidence of both tears and laughter in my class during story time only reinforces my confidence in the value of reading to a child each day. I urge you ever so strongly to make reading to your child a regular feature of your day, a part of the daily routine that involves moments alone with each other and the pleasure of books.

Probably the most enjoyable way to read to your child is at bedtime. It is a nice time to curl up on the bed with him and share a pleasant experience. Be sure to sit with your child on your lap or close beside you—your arm will fit nicely around him and still allow you to hold the book—so that he can see the pages as you read.

Reading to your child is also your chance to be the actor or actress you may have been too inhibited to be. Give the various characters in the stories different voices. Try different accents when they seem appropriate. Make spooky parts spooky. Use your imagination to make the book real and alive. Ham it up! Your child will be enthralled by the change in you, and you'll both have fun. I guarantee it!

In his book, *The Read-Aloud Handbook*, Jim Trelease describes books for you to read to your child. He explains that reading aloud awakens a child's sleeping imagination and improves language skills. By reading aloud to a child, you allow him to sample the excitement and pleasures he isn't quite ready or willing to accomplish on his own.

Orville Prescott, author of *A Father Reads To His Children*, puts it this way: "Few children learn to love books by themselves. Someone has to lure them into the wonderful world of the written word; someone has to show them the way."

When To Start and What To Read

When should you start reading to your child? Virtually as soon as he is born! Until he is six or seven months old, it doesn't even matter *what* you read, only that you *do* read. At this point, you are simply allowing your child to get accustomed to the rhythmic sound of your reading voice. He will quickly come to associate reading books with a peaceful and secure time of the day.

When your child nears his first birthday, look for books which stimulate sight and hearing—books with lots of color and different sounds. At first, books with simple illustrations are best. Mother Goose rhymes are fun because of the rhythm and rhyming. Keep a book in your child's crib and playpen, and a few next to his car seat.

With a toddler, word books are great. They can help introduce him to names of objects in his world. He'll love to repeat new word names until he knows them. Then he will delight in supplying you with the names of objects you point to. You can also make a game of asking him to point out objects you "can't find" on a page. ("I wonder where the dog is. Do you see it?")

Keep in mind the importance of balancing reading with outside experiences. Expose your child to as many things, places, and people as possible. Visiting a farm where your child can pat a cow, hear ducks quack, and smell hay is far more educational (and fun!) than looking at a book about a farm. Seeing these things later in books will be exciting and enjoyable because they will have real meaning for him. For this reason, early books about animals, insects, cars, trucks and boats—things a child is likely to see in the world around him—are important. Both you and your child will be thrilled with the "it's just like in my book" exclamations!

Try to choose books which are exciting or interesting to your child, and don't spend too long reading. Keep it short, appropriate to the attention span of your child.

Introduce your preschooler to a great variety of books: nonfiction as well as fiction; wordless as well as those with stories; joke and riddle books; poetry; and fairy tales. And as you introduce new and varied books, be sure to let your child select the book to be read, more often than not.

The older your child gets, the longer his attention span will become, if you continue to read aloud to him. When you feel he is ready for a novel, Trelease's first choice "a thousand times over" is *James and the Giant Peach*, by Roald Dahl. I would also suggest Dahl's *The BFG*. Make a point of stopping each night at an exciting point in the story, to tantalize your child and leave him looking forward to more. Make reading the treat it is!

How long after your child is reading well by himself should you continue reading aloud? For as long as you can—right up through middle school years. Oftentimes families will read exciting adventure stories aloud together or select books that are a bit advanced to read to older children. Try reading *Treasure Island* or *The Wind in the Willows* to older children. You may eventually switch over from a read aloud time to a quiet time where the whole family reads to themselves, sharing special passages aloud afterward. This is a good family experience, showing children that one never gets too old to read, and also opening up ideas for family discussion.

Not only is reading with your child fun and relaxing, but it is also a wonderful way to introduce words, expand his vocabulary. Reading to your child also creates the opportunity to talk about things. When you've finished for the night, or while you're in the car, you can ask your child questions like, "What do you think you'd do if you were in _____'s place?" "How do you feel about people who _____?" "Do you ever think about that?" These are just starter questions that can initiate some wonderful conversations. You will find more question ideas throughout this chapter.

You can help your child consider particular values, evaluate various points of view, question the way things are, and wonder aloud about growing up and all the choices and changes that lie ahead.

If possible, take your child to the library on a regular basis. Make choosing and reading new books an exciting experience. Book clubs can also be a fun way to obtain new stories. Books at the appropriate level for your child come in the mail (and we *all* love to get mail!) on a regular basis. For a school-age child, book club orders which teachers hand out are perhaps one of the least expensive ways to purchase books, and they offer many award-winners and old favorites.

What Kind of Questions Should I Ask?

Once upon a time, there was a girl named Little Red Riding Hood. Remember that one? My favorite part is where the wolf is lying in Grandma's bed, frilly nightcap on his head, spectacles resting on his long snout, and Little Red Riding Hood says, "Oh, Grandma, what big teeth you have!" The wolf jumps out of the bed crying, "The better to eat you with!"

I'm going to use that story to help introduce you to a group of questions and a method of classifying them called "Bloom's Taxonomy of the Cognitive Domain." Thinking skills exist on various levels of complexity, and once you are aware of these levels, you can challenge your child to s-t-r-e-t-c-h his mind with different kinds of questions. You will recognize the types of questions as ones you already ask your child, but it is useful to see the progression in complexity, for it helps make expectations more realistic.

The questions below go with the story of Little Red Riding Hood, but you will see how they might be applied to any story or subject area.

KNOWLEDGE. This first level deals with the basic recall of facts, the ability to simply take in information.
- Where did Grandma live?
- Who rescued Little Red Riding Hood?
- What did the wolf do with Grandma?

COMPREHENSION. This and the first level form the foundation blocks for all other thinking. Comprehension means understanding what is going on in a story.
- Tell me what the story was about.
- Why was Little Red Riding Hood going to her Grandma's?
- What was the wolf like?

APPLICATION. At this point in *Bloom's Taxonomy*, the child begins to use the information and apply it to other situations. He begins to create original thoughts.
- What would you have done if you had found a wolf in your Grandma's bed?

- If you are stopped by a stranger on your way to school, what should you do?
- If the wolf came to your Grandma's house, where would he have hidden her?

ANALYSIS. This level deals with categorizing, filling-in, and analyzing similarities and differences.
- How is the wolf in the story like a real wolf? How is he different?
- Compare the way the wolf tricked Grandma and the way he tricked Little Red Riding Hood.
- Which characters in the story were good? Which were bad?
- Have you ever tried to trick someone using a different voice or a costume? Did it work?

SYNTHESIS. At this level, the child redesigns, invents, or creates something new from things he already knows.
- Retell the story with a skit, puppet show, or song.
- Can you think of a different title for the story? How about a different ending?
- What did Little Red Riding Hood write in her diary that night?
- Retell the story from the wolf's point of view.

EVALUATION. This, the highest level of thinking skills, deals with making judgments where there is no definite right answer. The child must make a decision and be prepared to support it with valid reasoning.
- If you had been Little Red Riding Hood, would you have stopped to talk to the wolf? Why or why not?
- Was Little Red Riding Hood a good little girl? Why?
- When Little Red Riding Hood first saw a funny-looking Grandma, what should she have done? Why?

Talk with your child about this and other stories you read together. Start with the simpler questions and work your way up. You will be able to tell at which level your child is functioning by the answers he gives. Don't push for answers to the harder questions, but help your child think about them. Thinking out answers and expressing them clearly aren't easy skills to learn. They require a lot of patient talking and listening on your part. Whenever possible, let your child know, "Hey, that's a good thought!"

How to Encourage Reading

The key to teaching a child to read is not only teaching him how to read, but also teaching him to want to read, and that is where parents play a vital role.

If I were to mention the "golden arches" to you, or begin singing, "You deserve a break today," chances are you would know immediately what I was referring to and would sing the next line of the song, ending with the name of that well-known chain of restaurants—McDonald's.

Over the years, we have been bombarded with new and clever jingles, irresistible faces—all telling us that the quick answer to our hunger problems is McDonald's. Somehow the message succeeded in luring us in to their thousands of restaurants across the nation to buy their specialty foods because, let's face it, McDonald's is BIG, it's SUCCESSFUL.

Jim Trelease, author of *The Read-Aloud Handbook*, says we as parents and teachers need to approach teaching children to read the same way McDonald's approaches selling the public on its food. We need to "advertise" books over and over again, singing new praises, enjoying them ourselves, and giving "book commercials" to show our enthusiasm for reading.

I don't think any of us question the value of learning to read, but teaching a child to read needs to start long before school begins. A child should be exposed to books and the pleasures of reading while he is still young enough to want to imitate what he sees and hears.

Reading Activities

➡ Read to your child every day. A bedtime story is not only fun and a chance for learning, but it also makes going to bed a pleasant event.

➡ If you have an old typewriter, let your child use it to write with. A child will recognize letters before he can form them on his own.

➡ With a beginning reader, write down short stories your child dictates to you. He will enjoy having you read his own words back to him much more than he might enjoy a story about someone he does not know. Encourage him to illustrate his stories.

➡ Buy several different children's magazines at the supermarket. See which one your child enjoys most, and subscribe to it. Subscriptions are not too expensive and your child will eagerly anticipate receiving his own mail and reading his magazine or having it read to him.

MAKING YOUR OWN BOOKS

There are lots of ideas for creating a variety of books your child will enjoy reading over and over.

 ➡ Use a book with blank pages, a scrapbook, a photo album with plastic sheets, or make your own book (see instructions below).

➡ Print or type a story your child has dictated. (When typing or printing, keep in mind how much you want on each page and leave space accordingly.)

➡ Illustrate with your child's own artwork, photos, or pictures your child cuts out of magazines.

➡ Use rubber cement whenever gluing paper to paper. This will eliminate rippled pages.

➡ Make a book *about your child!* He will love being the main character of a story. Use photos and pictures from magazines, or make your own illustrations. For a toddler, keep it simple, writing the story in the first person. "Hi. My name is _____. I live with _____. I like to _____ and _____." Include pages about the child's favorite color, animal, food, toy, and so on.

For a 5- or 6-year-old, try writing a story in the third person. "Once there was a little girl named _____. She lived with _____." And so on.

HOW TO MAKE A BOUND BOOK

❶ Fold together one piece of construction paper (cut to 8½" × 11") and as many sheets of typing paper as you want, keeping the construction paper on the outside.

❷ Stitch along the fold, through all sheets. You can stitch the pages on a sewing machine or by hand with a needle and doubled thread (see figure 1).

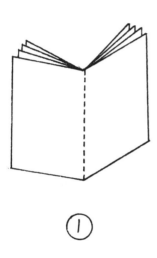

①

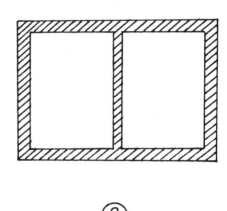

②

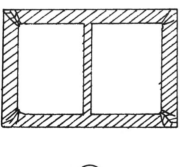

③

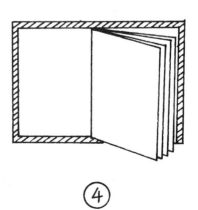

④

❸ Cut two pieces of cardboard, each approximately 5½″ × 6¾″.

❹ Lay the two pieces of cardboard on the wrong side of a piece of non-stretch fabric, approximately ¼″ apart. Cut the fabric 1″ larger on all sides (see figure 2).

❺ Apply a thin, watered layer of white glue to the back of the cardboard and replace on fabric as before, gluing the fabric to the covers.

❻ Next, apply glue to the 1″ excess of fabric and fold over onto the cardboard (see figure 3).

❼ Now, glue the construction paper and pages into the cover, closing the cover around the paper. The construction paper will neatly cover the turned-in edges of the fabric (see figure 4).

❽ Place waxed paper around the book and inside the front and back covers. Press under some heavy books until dry and flat.

❾ Fill with pictures, stories, products of your child's imagination!

Using the Newspaper

When my husband brings the paper in from the driveway every morning, he automatically goes for the sports section. I pretty much tend to take what's left, in whatever order it's in. I know I'll get to it all sooner or later.

There are many ways in which you can use the newspaper as a learning tool and a fun activity, even with a preschooler who is just beginning to learn sounds. The activities listed below are a starting point. Change or adapt them in any way you feel necessary to make them more appropriate for your child. Be ready to help if needed, and offer encouraging words.

Newspaper Activities

1 Read the comics to your child. Toddlers like ones with sound words like "slurp," "clunk," and "bleah!" (Exaggerate the sounds to make it extra funny.) Comics are also a good way to help an older child understand and appreciate humor.

2 Label sheets of paper "Happy" and "Sad." (Or draw happy and sad faces.) Have your child clip pictures (photos and/or comics) which fit one of these emotions, and paste them to the appropriate page.

3 Label different sheets of paper with headings like Living Room, Kitchen, Dining Room, Bedroom, Yard. (You may have to supply illustrations of each heading.) Have your child clip pictures of household objects and paste them on the appropriate pages. Let your child come up with other headings.

4 Label half-sheets of paper with the letters of the alphabet. Ask your child to find pictures of objects that start with these letters and paste them on the appropriate page. (This is far too much for one day. Before your child begins to tire of the project, stop him, praise his efforts, and put the pages aside for another day. Later, have your child show other family members what he's done so far, to supply incentive to complete the task later.)

5 Have your child clip and paste pictures of things that begin or end with the same sound.

6 Have your child clip and paste pictures of things that rhyme.

LEARNING
TO
READ

As I knocked on the door of my friends' house, I could see through the window, Lisa and Jason sitting on the living room floor. Lisa is the mother of 3-year-old Jason. They were looking through the newest *Sesame Street* magazine. Pencils and scissors lay on the carpet nearby. Cutting things out is one of Jason's favorite activities. While I was there, he cut out the "cards" for a game of "Concentration." We played two games, and I was fascinated by how many different skills are used in such a seemingly simple activity. Cutting with scissors is a difficult, but valuable exercise in small motor control. Matching pairs of cards requires visual discrimination and memory. To determine who won, we each had to count how many pairs of cards we had.

There is almost nothing as delightful to a child as having you to himself, knowing that you have chosen to spend time with him, doing something together. Working on activities, such as those described above, is an extremely valuable way to spend that time alone with your child. This chapter contains many more suggestions.

According to Nancy Larrick, author of *A Parent's Guide to Children's Reading*, a child's aptitude for reading is determined long before he enters kindergarten. She also makes the following, scary prediction: "Many children are already on the road to reading failure when they enter first grade." I would hesitate to make such a negative statement, and tend to believe that a parent *can* make a difference in his child's intellectual development for many years after his fifth birthday. But certainly *the earlier a child's parents become actively involved in his education, the better his chances for success.*

Dr. Dolores Durkin conducted studies on two groups of children—one in California, the other in New York City—to determine the impact of early reading on a child's later reading achievement. In the California study, she followed the progress of 49 children who had entered the first grade already knowing how to read. She compared their growth in reading to that of approximately 5,000 children who had entered first grade as non-readers at the same time. Dr. Durkin found that these 49 early readers, who were not necessarily any different from other children in intelligence or personality, stayed ahead of the other children for the five years during which the study was conducted. This raises the question whether children who learn to read later will catch up to early readers.

The second study included an experimental group of 30 early readers and a control group of 30 children who could not read when they entered first grade. The groups were matched for intelligence, so that intelligence could not be considered a factor in the results. Again, the reading achievement of the early readers was significantly higher, and remained so for the three years of the test.

How and why do some children learn to read before entering school? Dr. Durkin's research lead her to conclude that *the difference lay not in the children, but in the mothers of the children.* The mothers of the early readers acted on the belief that *trained teachers are not the only ones who can or should teach children to read.* These mothers provided a stimulating environment for their children, read to them, talked with them, explained word meanings, and helped their children learn to print.

But let us not put the responsibility solely on mothers. Both parents as well as other actively involved adults in a child's care can help provide the necessary warm, stimulating environment for early reading.

Reading Readiness

How can a parent best prepare his child to learn to read? By providing him with a variety of reading readiness activities which will help him develop the skills he needs in order to learn to read. Keep in mind that activities in nearly every other area of learning (art, oral language, physical education, and so on) also contribute to the development of a child's readiness to read. Also vital to the success of your efforts in teaching your child to read is the attitude discussed in chapter 3 which your child must gain from you—a belief that books are fun, and being read to is a treat!

If you find, after working on the following readiness activities, that your child is thirsty to learn more, and wants you to identify letters and words for him, you can feel comfortable continuing beyond these pre-reading activities. Be sure, too, that this is something you want to do, that working with your child is something you enjoy, because, as you know, children are very sensitive to underlying messages and feelings. Teaching a child to read requires considerable time and effort on your part, but it will be an immensely rewarding experience for you both.

If, on the other hand, your child shows no interest in learning the letters of the alphabet, continue offering readiness activities, first-hand experiences, and daily exposure to reading. Accept his needs as an individual. Pressuring him to learn before he is ready will only turn him off to reading, and will do more harm than good. Shared goals and shared enthusiasm always work better than one-sided demands.

Reading Readiness Activities

SERIATION (arranging objects in order following specific criteria or duplicating a pattern)

➡ Collect a set of 5 buttons (or boxes or blocks or circles of paper) of varying sizes. Ask your child to find the smallest one. Then, arrange the rest in order from smallest to largest, left to right. Discuss what you've done, mix the buttons up, and ask your child to find the largest button. See if he can arrange the buttons in order from largest to smallest.

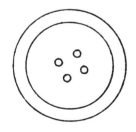 

➡ Make a pattern using toothpicks or dry cereal pieces, and have your child duplicate it.

➡ String different colored beads into a pattern and have your child duplicate the pattern exactly. Start with 3 or 4 beads per pattern, and add more when he is ready.

➡ Cut paper towel tubes into different sizes. Have your child arrange the pieces into a row from the shortest to the tallest.

MEMORY

➡ Ask your child to help you put away the groceries after your next trip to the store. Choose no more than five items for him to put away. When he is done, ask him if he can tell you what the five items were that he put away.

➡ Place several items on a table. Ask your child to pick up two objects you name, in the order you name them. Later, ask for three or four objects, in order.

➡ When making a can of soup, jello, or pudding, read the directions aloud first. Then ask your child to repeat them. "What should I do first?" "Now what?" Encourage your child to participate in the cooking.

➡ In the evening, go over the meals your child has eaten during the day, beginning with breakfast. See how well he remembers the foods he ate at each meal.

➡ Show your child a picture with many objects in it, and talk about the different things. Then put the picture away and ask your child to name as many of the details of the picture as he can remember. Make it fun by giving hints ("up in the corner"; "you always ask me to buy this for you"; "rhymes with _____").

➡ Place a number of objects on a table. Have your child look carefully at the objects for ten seconds, and then turn his back. Remove one of the objects. Ask him to look again to see if he can discover which has been removed. Add more objects, and change and rearrange the objects to make the game more difficult. This is a good activity for several children to play together. (One leaves the room, another removes an object, all stay very quiet when the child returns.)

➡ Draw a pattern on a chalkboard, or on a piece of paper, while your child watches. (Keep it simple and use geometric shapes.) Erase it, or remove it, and ask your child to draw it.

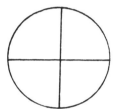 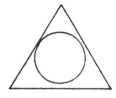 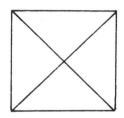

VISUAL DISCRIMINATION

➡ Using six pennies, line them up in the pattern: heads, tails, tails, tails, tails, heads. Point to the first penny and ask your child to find another one that looks just like it. Change the order; try using four heads and two tails, or use nickels, dimes, or quarters for variation.

➡ As you are driving or walking, point out a familiar traffic sign (STOP, YIELD, and so on), or a common store or gas station sign. Encourage your child to look for more of them. EXIT signs on an interstate give lots of opportunities to play this game. Have your child count how many he sees.

➡ Have your child tell you how things are alike or different. Compare pictures, houses, cars, people, anything.

➡ Cut out, in pairs, swatches of wallpaper or of fabric, and glue them onto index cards or pieces of cardboard for easy handling. Mix and have your child pair up the swatches. Later, you can use these for a memory game of concentration.

EYE-HAND COORDINATION AND MOTOR CONTROL

➡ Encourage your child to use his hands as much as possible to improve his manual dexterity. He should learn to dress himself as soon as possible. Let him turn pages in books you read together, handle different objects, play with clay and play-dough, cut with scissors, paint with a brush, hold a pencil, braid.

➡ Make a game of "basketball." Give your child a 3" diameter ball or beanbag, and have him try to throw it into a 10" diameter wastebasket or a large box. Have him start close and shoot from farther away as he improves.

➡ Using old magazines or newspapers, help your child look for and cut out pictures of different things and paste them onto blank pieces of paper by category. When you have a good number of pages, bind them together into a book. Some possible categories would be: dogs, houses, vegetables, different jobs. In addition to providing practice in small muscle control (cutting with scissors), this activity also helps a child learn to categorize.

➡ Drill holes into pieces of wood at least 1½" thick. Glue different size nuts over the holes. Have your child screw the screws into the correctly sized nuts on the board with a screwdriver. This is a good activity, a favorite of many!

➡ Help your child develop body coordination by practicing basic motor skills, like throwing, catching, kicking a ball, jumping rope, hopping on one or two feet, skipping, doing jumping jacks, and walking along a balance beam of some sort. (See chapter 9 for more ideas.)

➡ Encourage your child to use scissors. (Some children's scissors work much better than others. Try them yourself first.)

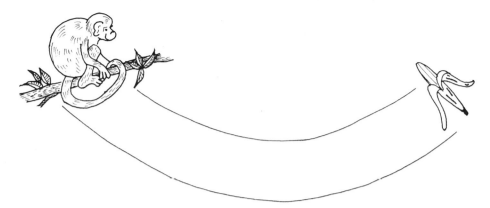

➡ Draw a monkey (or cut and paste one from a magazine), and a banana on the left and right sides respectively of a piece of paper. Connect the two with parallel lines drawn about 1″ apart. Ask your child to draw a line to "lead the monkey to the banana." (You can also draw people going to a house or to the park or to school, and so on or make the lines curve.)

➡ Show your child how to lace a shoe.

➡ Learning to track. Long before a child can read words, he can recognize and name pictures of objects. You can use this ability to help introduce your child to the idea of reading and moving his eyes in a left-to-right tracking motion. The sample below shows how you can make up or "rewrite" stories, nursery rhymes, and fairy tales using a combination of words and illustrations. You can draw your own pictures or cut them out of magazines, comics, etc. You might want to photocopy those pictures you need repeatedly. Before "reading" the story with your child, introduce him to the pictures you have used, so that he will be able to supply the right words later when he sees them.

As you read with your child, sit so that he can clearly see the page, and move your index finger under the words as you read. Go fairly slowly so that he will learn that each word you *say* belongs with a particular bunch of "squiggles." Your child will eventually recognize certain written words simply because he has seen and heard them repeatedly in these stories.

GEORGE'S NEW HOME

George was a little, yellow 🐦 . He lived in a cage in a big 🏠 with a 👦 named Loren, a 👧 named Carey, and their parents. In the 🏠 , there also live a 🐕 and a 🐈 .

George liked his family, but he grew tired of his cage. How he wished he could fly like the other 🐦🐦 he saw out the window! He would watch them for hours, flying from 🌳 to 🌳 , building 🪺 and carring food in their beaks.

One day the 🐈 climbed on a 🪑 near George's cage. "What's wrong?" asked the 🐈 . "You don't sing as much as you used to."

"I'm lonely," answered George. "I want to fly outside like other 🐦🐦 ." And he tipped his head toward the window.

"That's easy enough to fix," said the . "I'll open your

cage, and when the and come home from school, you

can fly out the !"

And that's just what George did!

The and were sad to see George leave, and tried

to catch him. But when the little sang so merrily to them

from the outside the , they could see that he was much

happier being free.

Now, every day, they put seed and bread out for

George and his friends. And every evening, as the sets,

George sits in a and sings a happy goodnight song to the

family in the

CATEGORIZATION

➡ While shopping in the produce section of the grocery store, discuss different criteria for categorizing or describing fruit (color, shape and size). Ask your child to find fruits that are red (or round or little). Choose a fruit and ask him to describe it using the three criteria.

➡ Let your child name the types of clothing as you sort or fold the laundry. Have him tell you which pile each item belongs in, such as Daddy's shirts, sister's socks, his overalls.

➡ Place a number of objects on a table, all but one of which are related in an obvious way. Have your child pick out the one object that doesn't fit with the others, and ask him to explain *why* he chose the object he did. (Example: an eraser, a pencil, an apple, and a piece of paper.)

➡ Give your child the name of a category such as "Animals," and have him name as many different kinds of animals as he can. For older children, have them name animals beginning with a specific letter.

LANGUAGE/VOCABULARY DEVELOPMENT

➡ With even the smallest infant, you can "play" with lots of talk. Tell him what you are doing, and why, as you bathe and dress him. Set him in the room in which you are working and explain what you are doing, step by step. TALK, TALK, TALK, and sing too!

➡ With children who have begun to talk, word books help you introduce hundreds of words. Picture books without words allow the creation of whatever story the child wants to invent to accompany the illustrations. Listen attentively to these stories.

➡ Help your child become aware of the many possible positions of and relationships between objects, such as: right, left, forward, backward, top, through, over, under, after, pair, behind, in front of, corner, center, next to, inside, outside, between, whole, part. Ask position questions about pictures or in the grocery store: "What is next to the soup?" "What is over the books?"

➡ To help your child get a feeling for the rhythm and music in language, sing songs and say nursery rhymes to and with him. Encourage his participation in such language experiences. It will help him enjoy them more.

➡ A 3-year-old is a steady talker, and will talk not only to people, but to cats, to dolls, to himself. Turn off the radio or T.V. so that your child can carry on conversations or monologues without "electronic competition."

➡ Make a point of providing your child with a full and accurate vocabulary, instead of limiting it to generalities. For example, when your child spots a dog, avoid general observations like, "Yes, there's a dog." Instead, say, "Yes, that dog is an Irish Setter."

➡ Encourage use of complete sentences. If your child says, "We go to store," gently redirect him by saying, "Yes, we are going to the store," and encourage him to repeat the sentence correctly. Do not, however, correct him in front of others; children are as sensitive to this as adults are.

➡ Using pictures or actual people as a starting point, talk about different jobs and the equipment used in them. Again, encourage specific terms such as a "bucket loader" rather than "truck."

OBSERVATION

➡ When taking a walk with your child, look for things made of wood or paper or glass or metal or cement. Choose a different substance each day.

➡ While your child is in the bathtub, give him various objects to play with and help him discover their different properties, such as which sink, which float, and why? Try objects such as a wooden spoon, a metal spoon, a cork, plastic bottles and containers, and a sponge.

➡ Given different size jars or cups and a large number of walnuts (or other fairly large objects), have your child guess how many walnuts it would take to fill each container. Then have him fill and count.

➡ When discovering things with your child, ask him questions which will force him to notice details. For instance, when you describe a dog as an Afghan, instead of just "dog," ask your child what color its fur is, what kind of fur it has, if its ears flop or stand up, and if it is large or small.

➡ Look through a magazine and find three or four things pictured in it. Tell your child what they are and ask him to find and circle them or cut them out.

Introducing the Alphabet

You will know when your child is ready to learn the letters of the alphabet, because he will show a real interest in letters and will begin to recognize words. This interest *may* appear around the age of 3½, but it very well may not develop until the age of 4 or 5! It will be clear that he realizes that spoken words can also be written and that words on paper can also be spoken. He may point to words in a book and "read" a story of his own making. Although he can not yet read the words, he knows what they're for, and that's a giant step!

This is when you want to offer lots of exposure to the letters of the alphabet. Start with capitals. (You will help your child if you use the same lettering now, that you are going to use when teaching him to *write* later. An illustration is included in chapter 6, "Beginning to Print.") Neatly print a chart for your child's wall, or a long strip that will go around a corner! Use red or blue marker, rather than black, simply because colors seem to have an added appeal. At the same time, make a set of letter flashcards, using 3 × 5 index cards. Wood Smethurst, author of *Teaching Young Children to Read at Home*, suggests drawing a blue line along the bottom of each card. This way your child will always know which way to hold it to be sure it's right side up. Magnetic letters for the refrigerator are also a great investment.

Activities

➡ Work on one letter at a time. You might want to begin with the letters in your child's name.

➡ Practice writing each new letter in sand or fingerpaint. *Actual writing of letters should be strictly voluntary at this point.*

➡ Help your child form the letter from clay or play-dough.

➡ Let your child help you make cookie dough and then create cookies in the shapes of the letters he has learned.

➡ Cut letters out of sandpaper and glue them to cardboard for your child to trace with his fingers.

➡ Make a large letter out of paste on construction paper. Have your child stick cereal, beans, dried noodles or buttons on the still wet paste.

➡ Look for each new letter on cereal boxes, on signs, in the newspaper, and in books.

➡ Make a "tree" on which to hang letters as they are learned; or put letters on a notebook binder ring once your child can recognize them with ease. He can clip the ring around his beltloop or hang it in a place where he can look at it easily and often, and *see* how much he has learned.

➡ Once your child has learned to recognize 3 or 4 letters, play a game with the letter cards you made. Using the letters he knows, and one or two new ones, put them in a pile, face up. Each card your child can name, he gets to keep!

Remember to take it slowly! Learn new letters only as your child is ready. You are working on the foundation of his reading skills. It may take 2 months, 6 months, or even a year for your child to learn to recognize all the letters. That's OK!

Once your child has learned all the capital letters, you can introduce him to the lowercase letters. Make a chart and letter cards like you did with the capital letters. Start by introducing those letters which closely resemble their capitals: c, k, o, s, p, t, u, v, w, x, y, z. Writing letters on paper should still be voluntary. Offer the same type of activities as you did with capital letters.

➡ Make a matching game with pairs of cards made of the capital and lowercase form of each letter. Play with those he has learned, but don't keep score.

➡ Start an alphabet book, allowing a page for each letter. Cut out capitals and lower case letters from magazines and newspapers. Leave the majority of the page for phonics activities later.

➡ If you haven't already done so, make a book from a story your child dictates to you. Make the title of the first book, "_____'s Book," using the child's name. On all other books he dictates or later writes himself, his name should be printed on the cover as the author.

Sight Words

Although I feel an understanding of phonics is an essential part of learning to read, (at least for *most* children), learning some words by sight is inevitable, necessary, and useful. Once your child can recognize the letters of the alphabet (both capitals and lowercase), learning sight words provides him with a reason for having learned the letters and for now learning their sounds. *If he is interested*, let him choose one new word each day that he would like to see in print. Make flash cards. Start with a 5-letter maximum length and move on to longer words only when your child seems ready or if he has a strong desire to learn a particular word.

Activities

➡ You can punch holes in the sight word cards and keep them on a single notebook binder ring. Hang the ring with the cards on a hook, somewhere where you are likely to see them, and review them often. Children enjoy seeing the cards accumulate. You might want to have two rings—one for words you have introduced and one for words your child knows and can read without hesitation. It's a very concrete way for a child to see his vocabulary growing.

➡ Put signs and labels on things around the house, in your child's room especially (door, bed, book, mirror). Better yet, if he has been learning to write letters, guide him in making his own signs.

➡ Have your child copy the words and thus write as well as read them, if he has started writing already.

➡ Using 10 cards at a time, have your child read them as quickly as possible. If he makes a mistake, correct him and have him repeat the word correctly, then try again. Don't dwell on a mistake.

➡ Below is *Harry Forgan's Initial Sight Word List.* This list, like the better-known *Dolch Word List,* offers a starting point for a child who already recognizes the letters of the alphabet and is learning their sounds.

Use the list to make flash cards (5″ × 7″ index cards work well) and include pictures with the words whenever possible. Make it fun for your child to learn to read the words! Look for them in books, on signs, etc.

FORGAN'S INITIAL SIGHT WORD LIST

me	boy	mommy	child's own name		
we	you	daddy	pet (or pet's name)		
I	she	there	name of favorite toy		
it	eat	they	name of favorite food		
he	our	them	name of favorite color		
is	one	girl	friend (or friend's name)		
am	out	could	sister (or sister's name)		
up	all	jump	brother (or brother's name)		
in	get	about	which	when	good
by	her	their	bring	this	your
my	new	would	some	give	with
a	but	think	then	said	look
as	use	work	play	soon	very
to	his	from	were	that	come
at	the	went	make	like	take
of	run	have	came	been	can
go	are	see	will	has	did
be	had	was	saw	not	for
or	and	on	so	do	

Challenge your child to recognize them. Play innocent sometimes and say, "Oh, I know I've seen that word before, but I can't remember what it is. Do you know?" Your child will love being able to help you out. He will also enjoy reading his new words to other members of the family.

➡ Arrange a few of the word cards in a sentence for your child to read. Let him do the same for you.

SHE	WILL	COME	SOON

Phonics

Phonics! Why not "fonix," or "fonicks"? Where is the sense in this language of ours? It can be so exasperating, especially when a child asks you to explain its inconsistencies. Annoying as it may be, it is our language, and we do have some rules which work pretty well a good part of the time.

Phonics deals with listening to and hearing the sounds that make up words. It also concerns itself with learning to associate letters with the sounds they make, and thus learning to read and to write the words as well.

While no two authorities totally agree on when and how to teach phonics, the prerequisites seem to be clear: good speech and oral vocabulary, good visual and auditory discrimination, recognition of the letters of the alphabet, and good motor control for writing.

If your child is in school and beginning to read, you will want to speak to his teacher to find out how you can best work with your child to reinforce what he is learning in school. If your child is not yet in school, but you feel he is ready and eager to begin reading, you can go ahead and introduce him to phonics.

If you have an older child who has trouble reading and whose foundation in phonics is inadequate, you may be able to help him pick up the skills he missed earlier by going back and starting from the beginning.

In preparation for working on phonics, you should make a poster and/or a set of flash cards. On each, write a letter in capital and lowercase form, and draw or glue a picture of something familiar that begins with that letter. Encourage your child to help you find the pictures. Below is a list of possible words to use to help your child associate letters with their sounds.

Aa — apple	Jj — jar	Ss — snake
Bb — boy	Kk — key	Tt — table
Cc — cat	Ll — ladder	Uu — umbrella
Dd — dog	Mm — man	Vv — vase
Ee — elephant	Nn — nail	Ww — woman
Ff — fish	Oo — octopus	Xx — x-ray
Gg — girl	Pp — penny	Yy — yoyo
Hh — hat	Qq — quarter	Zz — zipper
Ii — Indian	Rr — ring	

Consider your child's interests when choosing words. It may be more helpful for him to use "violin" instead of "vase," or "grapes" instead of "girl." *Choose words that are meaningful to your child.*

You will also want to cut up index cards to make small cards or purchase white ceramic tiles (1" square) on which to write individual letters of the alphabet. Write the consonants in black, and the vowels in a different, contrasting color. This is a good time to introduce the terms "consonant" and "vowel" to your child. Consonants are all those letters in the alphabet besides the vowels (a, e, i, o, u). Explain that every word must have at least one vowel, but the number of consonants can vary.

In making the letter cards, use capitals, and make three or four of each letter so that later you can build words and sentences with them. You may want to buy a chalkboard if you don't already have one. It will be extremely useful as well as fun for your child.

Although theories and methods of teaching phonics vary, here are some of the basic concepts involved and some game ideas to help teach them.

Start With Consonants

First of all, be sure to pronounce words carefully at home. Encourage your child to say words correctly. If he has difficulty with a particular word or sound, have him watch your mouth as you say it aloud and silently.

Most experts agree on starting phonics with the consonants. Introduce only five or so at first, adding new letters/sounds *only* after the first five have been mastered. Be careful when explaining the sound a letter makes. Try to keep the sound as brief as possible. For example, when introducing the sound of the letter "p," don't say "puh." Try instead to produce only a puff of air. Remember, your child is an imitator and will exaggerate wherever you do.

CONSONANT ACTIVITIES

➡ Using your alphabet cards, set out those your child knows or is working on. Say a word and have him pick out the letter whose sound is heard at the beginning of that word.

➡ Have your child cut from a magazine, pictures of things which begin with a particular sound. Have him glue them to the appropriate page in the alphabet book he started earlier.

➡ Say a word and have your child tell you more words that begin with that sound.

➡ Point to objects or pictures and have your child tell or write the beginning sound or letter.

➡ Play a game of initials of people you both know. "Who is J.T.?"

➡ Using the alphabet cards, let your child "win" each card for which he can think of a word beginning with that letter.

➡️ Label paper bags with different letters your child has learned and perhaps the one on which he is currently working. Give him an assortment of supermarket items (or other objects) whose names begin with those letters. Ask your child to place each object in the appropriate bag.

SHORT VOWELS AND WORD FAMILIES

 ➡️ Play rhyming games with your child. "I'm thinking of a word that rhymes with up" or say two words and ask your child if they rhyme or not.

➡️ When your child is comfortable with the concept of rhyming (the idea that the beginnings of the words differ, but the endings are the same), you can introduce "word families." These are short words with one short vowel sound in the middle. The "at" family, for instance, would include words like bat, cat, fat, hat, and so on. Other families include: -ap, -an, -ack, -and, -ad, -en, -end, -el, -ed, -in, -ip, -it, -ill, -ig, -ot, -ock, -op, -un, -up, -ud, -ut.

➡️ Encourage your child to discover how many words he can make in each family. Have him use the individual letter cards or tiles to create one word and then new ones by replacing the first consonant with a different one.

➡️ Use magnetic letters to spell a new "mystery" word on the refrigerator each day. Make it one from the word family you plan to work on that day.

➡️ Present (on the chalkboard or paper, or using letter cards) pairs of words which differ only in their first letter. Have your child read the two words to you. (Ex. can/pan; sit/bit and so on.)

➡️ Spell out two or more words with letter cards or tiles, and ask your child to point to the one you say.

STARTING TO WRITE

Once your child can correctly associate letters with their normal sounds (he will eventually have to learn the exceptions), you should encourage him to start printing letters and words. Have paper readily available, along with pencils, pens, and a chalkboard. (Refer to chapter 6 for help in teaching your child to form letters.) *Don't worry about spelling at this point!* You don't want to discourage these first, exciting attempts to communicate in writing.

DIFFERENT ENDINGS

Once your child feels comfortable and can easily decode short words like those in the families listed, you can introduce words with different endings. Help him look at the end of the words to notice the difference between words like: mad/mat; pen/pet).

Point out how important it is to *look through the whole word.* While two words may start the same, their endings can be different.

When you feel he is ready, you can introduce *blends* where the sounds of two letters blend together, as "cl" in clock, clothes, and clay. Other blends include fl-, tr-, sl-, pl-, sp-, st-, pr-, br-, bl-.

LONG VOWELS

Up to now, your child has dealt with short vowel sounds and has learned to decode nearly any short word you can write. They follow a rule which you should point out to him once he has grasped the concept: *Usually when a word is short and has only one vowel in the middle, that vowel sound will be short.* To review: short "a" is the sound heard in "cat"; short "e" is the sound heard in "bed"; short "i" is the sound heard in "big"; short "o" is the sound heard in "hot"; and short "u" is the sound heard in "cup."

When your child is ready, go on to the long vowel sounds, beginning with long "e." Point out that a *long vowel sound is one where the vowel says its name.* Long "e" is usually spelled "ee," as in three, feet, sheet, meet, keep, teeth, week.

LONG "E" ACTIVITY

➡ Start with a word such as "seed" and ask your child to change "seed" into "feed." Either a chalkboard, a piece of paper, or cards on which individual letters are written will work well. Now ask, "Can you make "feed" into "feel"? And so on, changing either the beginning or ending sound to make new words.

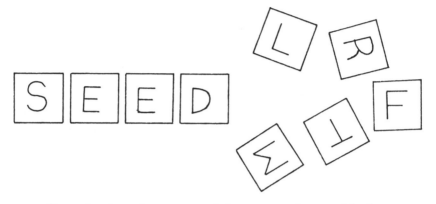

Spend a few days on each long vowel sound before moving on to a new one. Be sure your child has caught on to the sound and the letters involved, and feels sure of himself in dealing with them. Then introduce another vowel sound, remembering to review the old ones, as well.

If you sense frustration here or at any point, backtrack to something your child is comfortable with. This isn't a race and there are no deadlines to meet. Your child will let you know when it is time to move ahead again.

The remaining long vowel sounds are usually spelled with two vowels, with the long vowel coming first, and a second letter, usually a silent "e," coming at the end of the word.
- long "a" spelled a—e as in "cake"
- long "i" spelled i—e as in "five"
- long "o" spelled o—e as in "nose"
- long "u" spelled u—e as in "rule"

Sometimes the two vowels come next to each other, as in "boat" or "meat." In most cases, again it is the first vowel that is long. The second rule to tell your child is: *When two vowels go walking, the first one does the talking.* (In other words in "boat," you hear the first "o," but not the second "a".)

LONG VOWEL ACTIVITY

➡ Make special letter cards or tiles for silent "e" by writing them in a different color from your consonants and vowels.

➡ Present your child with the word "cut." It's a short word with one vowel in the middle, so the vowel is short. But if you add an "e," the word becomes "cute." It now has two vowels, so the first is long. You have a totally different word. You can come up with many more such pairs: bit/bite; rat/rate; rob/robe. Encourage your child to find more such pairs.

The third rule to present to your child is: *When a vowel comes at the end of a short word, the vowel is usually long.* (Examples: hi, we, go, no, he, so.) Point out that sometimes, "y" acts as a vowel, usually producing a long "i" sound (try, fly), or a long "e" sound (happy, easy).

In talking about long vowel sounds, your child will soon notice that there are other spellings of each.
• Long "a" is sometimes written "ai" or "ay" (rain, day).
• Long "e" is sometimes written "ea" (seat).
• Long "i" is sometimes written "igh" (night), or "y" at the end of a word (dry).
• Long "o" is sometimes written "oa" (boat), "ow" (slow), or "o" at the end of a word (go).
• Long "u" is sometimes written "ew" (flew).

The nice part about these alternative spellings is that except for "igh," they follow either Rule 2 or Rule 3.

Help your child realize that at first he may have to try two or three different spellings for a word until he gets the right one. Assure him that before long he will remember which spelling is correct for each word.

There remain some other vowel sounds that are fairly common, and that you will want to cover with your child. There are the sounds of "oi" or "oy" as in boil, boy; "aw," "au," or "all" as in saw, haul, ball; the sound of "ar" as in car; "oo" as in moon; "oo" as in book; "ow" or "ou" as in cow, out; and "ur," "er," "ir," and "or" as in turn, her, girl, and work.

This leaves us with *digraphs*—those combinations of letters which make new sounds, such as "sh," "ph," "ch," "wh," "th" (hard as in "think," soft as in "this"), or ending digraphs like -ck, or -ng (truck, ring).

Take your time introducing all these sounds. There's no rush to learn them right away. The more your child reads and practices writing, the more aware he will become of all the different spellings and sounds. Much of this really is a process of discovery—especially the many exceptions to the rules. Part of your role will simply be to answer questions calmly, and present new concepts very gradually.

MORE VOWEL ACTIVITIES

➡ Have your child find in a magazine, and circle, words with a particular vowel sound, digraph, or consonant blend.

➡ Have him cut out and paste onto paper, words or pictures of things with the same vowel sounds.

➡ Ask your child to listen for and name the vowel sounds in words you say aloud.

➡ Once your child feels comfortable with both the consonant and vowel sounds, and can write easily, dictate words for him to spell on a chalkboard or on paper. Begin with simple words. Say them slowly, and encourage your child to listen *through* the word to pick out the beginning sound, the vowel sound, and the ending sound.

BEGINNING
TO
PRINT

Doors are opening on a whole new world as your child learns to read. The black squiggles in his books begin to take on new meaning as he realizes that they stand for words he knows. As he begins to recognize individual letters of the alphabet, and their sounds, he sees that they are what make up the words in his books. Suddenly he feels an urge to write his own letters and words so he can say things on paper, too.

When should you begin encouraging your child to write? There's little reason to begin until he has learned to recognize the letters of the alphabet and their sounds. Before he reaches this point, however, you can be helping him practice activities involving small muscle control, so that when he is ready, his hands will have the necessary coordination to produce letters on paper.

It's important to remember that your child's first attempts at writing will be like his first attempts to feed himself—clumsy! But they will be exciting to him! A certain sense of power, self-confidence and independence will accompany his growing ability to communicate with others. Until your child can reproduce letters easily from memory, don't worry about neatness, size, reversals, or misspelled words. There will be plenty of time for that. Guide him, whenever possible, to form letters correctly, but most of all, you want writing to be a fun game.

Which hand?

John was a fifth grader with some behavior problems and the most illegible handwriting of any student I had ever taught. He was an exceptionally bright child, and I worked hard to keep his brain challenged!

The subject of John's handwriting came up routinely at parent conferences. It was not until one of the last meetings that his mother finally confessed to me the probable reason behind the illegible handwriting. When he was first learning to print, John tried repeatedly to hold his pencil with his left hand. His mother, conforming to the old view that writing with the left hand is simply not desirable or correct, literally forced him to learn to write with his right hand.

Research conducted in recent years concerning the manner in which the brain functions has made it clear that there is a reason for a child preferring one hand over the other. To deny his natural preference has to be confusing to his brain and frustrating to the child.

If you are not sure which hand your child naturally prefers, you can give him five or six different tasks several times a week for two or three weeks. Keep track of his hand preference each time he performs each task, and at the end of several weeks, a definite preference should be obvious. Suggested tasks are: using scissors, combing hair, eating, reaching for an object, pounding a hammer, opening a door, throwing a ball.

As you keep track of the results, be sure to write them down. Otherwise, human nature being what it is, you may "see" what you wish, rather than the actual preference. If your child is left-handed, don't make a big deal about it, and by all means, *don't try to change a natural dominant hand preference.*

HOLDING THE PENCIL

Once you have determined which hand your child uses more easily and naturally, help him learn to hold his crayon or pencil in a comfortable grip. While the accepted grip is to hold the pencil between the thumb and index finger, the pencil resting against the third finger, research has shown that grip has little effect on either speed or legibility of writing. For some reason, I've always used my thumb and two fingers on the pencil, allowing it to rest on my fourth finger. As my penmanship doesn't seem to have suffered, what appears to be most important about grip, is that a person is comfortable with it.

You want to remind your child to hold the pencil above the sharpened area. With a left-hander, it is important to encourage him to grip the pencil even higher. This helps him from having to curve or hook his wrist in order to see his writing. Reminding the left-hander to keep his elbow close to his body will also help prevent this hooked-wrist position.

PREWRITING ACTIVITIES

Before beginning to work on the letters of the alphabet, there are some preliminary exercises which you should be working on with your child to help him develop the motor control he will need to write. Ideally, you have been encouraging your child all along to draw and thus practice lines similar to those below. Until your child is capable of producing these lines without too much difficulty, he will have a hard time reproducing the shapes involved in the letters of the alphabet.

 ➡ Try the following activities and make pictures and games (Tic-Tac-Toe, for example) out of the practice. Use big pieces of paper sometimes, and smaller pieces at other times, to vary the task.

❶ Straight lines: ||₁₁|₁|

❷ Horizontal bars: ⁻ ⁻ _ ⊥ † ⊬ ⧕

❸ Squares: | | ⊓ □

❹ Circles: ◯ ○

❺ Part circle: (◁⊃ ☻⊃ ∩ C

❻ Slanted lines: / ∧ ⋀ △ ✕

❼ Hooks: ⌐ ⌡ ⅋

➡ To improve eye-hand coordination, create exercises like the one below. The paths from one thing to another should be 1½″ to 2″ wide. Start with a straight path and then try ones with curves. Find humorous or enticing pictures in comics or magazines, and glue them to the beginning and end of each path. The object of the exercise is to draw a line directly along the middle of the path. It requires concerted effort to draw a line equidistant from both sides of the path.

Forming Printed Letters

Once your child is ready to learn to write, start by teaching him to write his name. This will help nurture his enthusiasm. It is a good idea to have him begin on primary wide-lined paper. Several studies have shown that using this wide-lined paper improves a child's performance in forming letters.

Research also indicates that *children prefer adult pencils,* and do not write any better with the fat, beginner's pencils so often used in schools.

Your child should begin with printing. It is not only more like the type in books, but it is also more easily learned. Usually at the end of second grade or during the third grade, your child will be introduced to cursive handwriting. This seems to be by tradition, as there is no research which shows that cursive is more legible or faster than printing.

Below is one style of printing you can follow. There are other styles which vary slightly, but none has proven better than another. There is support for the idea that more effective teaching of writing includes *demonstration and verbal instruction* on letter formation. Let the arrows guide you in forming letters and have your child watch. Encourage him to verbalize what he is doing as he writes each letter on his paper. Keep in mind, too, that *copying* is a more valuable learning tool than *tracing*. If your child is uncomfortable following the order suggested by the arrows, and if he can form a letter using a slightly different method, let it go! I doubt if *anyone* forms all his letters in the manner shown. I know I don't. This is simply a guide, a starting point.

During this early phase of learning to write, you needn't be concerned about errors such as letters which are reversed or made incorrectly, or mistakes in the order of letters in a word. Don't worry at this point about size consistency, or spacing either. Keep in mind that we are not discussing penmanship at this point. Your goal is to clearly introduce good habits in printing, setting the stage for later instruction in penmanship. Learning to print involves so much more than recognizing letters. For some, fine motor control will come long after a child's desire to "write."

You might want to follow the order for introducing letters suggested in one of the handwriting workbooks by Scott, Foresman & Co. You will see that letters which are similar in formation are taught together.

1 l, i

2 L, H, F, E, I, T, t

3 h, n, m, r

4 U, u

5 D, P, B, b, p

6 O, o, C, c, a, d, q

7 G, e

8 g, f, S, s

9 J, j

10 X, x, V, v, W, w, y

11 N, A, Z, z, K, k

12 M, Y, R, Q

LANGUAGE: HAVING FUN WITH WORDS

The First Step:
Developing a Good Vocabulary

I think we all, at some time, have heard a parent ask a preschooler, "Do you want more wa-wa?" or "See the bow-wow?" instead of "Would you like some water?" or "Do you see the dog?" Perhaps you find you must admit doing the same thing. While baby talk may seem cute when a child is first learning to talk, to respond in and use such language, instead of using correct and adult English, only serves to perpetuate the baby talk, and minimize the child's development of a large and rich vocabulary.

As parents, you have a great opportunity to influence your child's vocabulary, and thus his success in reading, speaking, and written communication. The skills are unquestionably linked. *The greater a child's vocabulary, the greater his chances of understanding what he hears and reads.* A larger vocabulary will also mean better expression in writing.

I like the way Nancy Larrick, author of *A Parent's Guide to Children's Reading,* explains that a child can't develop good verbal ability on his own. "He needs someone who knows language better than he does and who is willing to play a pleasant game of conversation with him."

A child's (like anyone's) vocabulary is built through experience. The more he experiences, the more words he will run into and learn to use. And that is the proof of the pudding—when a child correctly uses what was once a new and strange word, you know he has learned it.

You can help your child increase his vocabulary by exposing him to as many different things as possible. Read to him, talk to him, take him places, show him things, and do things together. Visit a bank, the post office, the courthouse, a food processing plant, museums, the zoo, an airport. Discuss the visit with others afterwards, making a point of repeating new words until they become familiar enough for the child to use himself.

Take advantage of odd moments to introduce new words. For example, the next time you mist your plants, explain their need for a certain amount of *humidity*, instead of simply saying that they need to be sprayed with water. Remind him of the humidity in the bathroom when someone takes a shower. Explain that it is the amount of water or moisture (another good word) in the air. Listen for the term to be used on the weather report and read about it in the weather section of the newspaper.

There is a large vocabulary that exists mainly on signs found on doors, buildings, and vehicles. When you see one, find out if your child knows what it says, and most important, what it means. You should be extra careful to be sure he recognizes signs like: Danger, Poison, High Voltage, No Trespassing, Private, Beware of Dog, Combustible, Out of Order.

Oral Language

Parents provide models of grammar. Until I went to college in California, I'd spent all but six months of my life growing up in Connecticut. Where we live now, in Arkansas, my husband and I are still considered "Yankees." From time to time we have to smile as we catch ourselves starting to use a southern expression at home, such as "I'm fixin' to." How easy it is to pick up phrases and patterns of speech when one hears them all the time!

It is also easy to get used to those expressions which are grammatically incorrect, when they are used by many of the people around you. Often, since you understand perfectly well what the person means, you miss the fact that the phrase was not correct according to the rules of grammar taught in school. A child who is learning language has no idea what is or isn't correct English, and therefore, follows the lead of his parents, neighbors and silbings, and speaks as they do.

It is your role, as parent, to try to teach your child to use correct grammar from the beginning. It will make your child's job far easier when he gets to elementary school. As with anything, it is much more difficult to unlearn poor grammar habits than it is to learn them correctly at the start.

Listen to your child's grammar and help him correct any mistakes he repeatedly makes. With a young child still learning to put words together in sentences, you can help by simply restating his sentence correctly. For example, if he says, "I gots two cars," you might ask, "You have two cars?" or simply reaffirm what he said with, "Oh, you have two cars." He'll often notice your choice of words and repeat the sentence as you said it. This allows him to hear *himself* say what you did. He will often repeat a phrase three or four times in order to practice it. He takes learning to speak, seriously, and works hard at it.

With a child who is 4 years old or older, you can correct mistakes in the same non-judgmental, matter-of-fact way. You can also draw his attention to them and explain that there are correct ways to speak and write that you'd like to help him learn. You can point out appropriate phrases in books as examples, and remind him that when he gets older, teachers and employers will want him to use correct grammar. It will be easier if he learns the correct forms to begin with.

Common mistakes of grammar are:
• saying "I don't got" instead of "I don't have," or "I got" instead of "I have"
• using "ain't"
• using incorrect forms of verbs such as "I should've ate" instead of "I should've eaten"
• double negatives: saying "I don't have no" instead of "I don't have any" or "I have no"
• saying "I done" instead of "I did"
• using "good" when the adverb "well" should be used (Example: "I don't feel good." The correct sentence would be, "I don't feel well.")
• using colloquialisms

If you notice a mistake your child makes consistently, try to determine where he picked it up. It may be from his babysitter or playmates. Listen to your own speech to see if you might also be making the error. If you find that you, too, say "Can I?" when you should say "May I?", make it a joint effort with your child to help each other correct the mistake. The most important job is to learn to listen to and hear what you say. If you make the effort to improve your own grammar, you will be setting a great example for your child. The self-discipline required and the desire to improve are both worthwhile qualities to nurture.

Storytelling

In addition to talking to your child a lot, and reading to him every day, you can help him improve his language skills by telling stories to him. For many of us, that can be difficult at first. "What do I make up a story about?" If it's easier, start by telling old fairy tales and favorites like "The Three Bears," "The Three Pigs," and "The Ugly Duckling." If you're not sure of the plot, (I mixed "Snow White" with "Sleeping Beauty" for a while) don't worry too much about it. Your child won't know or care! If it makes you feel better, find a book and refresh your memory.

When you feel ready to make up your own story, I'd suggest making your child the main character. The story can be simple, about everyday things, or you can try adventures or fantasy. With a young child, be careful not to include action, ideas, or characters which might cause anxiety. Keep the plot fun or silly.

By telling stories rather than always reading them, you show your child another way in which words can be used. If he sees you making up stories, then, being a natural imitator, he will try himself. You can encourage him, by asking for his input in your stories. "What shall I tell a story about tonight?" "Where should he go?" "How will he get there?" "Who does he meet?" If he isn't ready to participate in the process, go ahead and make up the story yourself. He'll supply ideas when he's ready.

ORAL LANGUAGE ACTIVITIES

➡ To encourage your child's language development, ask him to observe, compare, and describe things around the house. For example, ask your child how the family dog (cat, fish, hamster) is like him. (It has a face. It has hair. It eats.) Talk about how the two are different. (The dog doesn't have hands. It doesn't wear clothes.)

➡ Play with your child making up rhymes, chants, and nonsense words. Sing songs together to make the sound of words fun, and the use of language an enjoyable experience.

➡ Encourage role playing. Ask your child to pretend he is a kitten, a fireman, or a mother. What sorts of things should he do to be that other person or thing? What sounds might he make? What would he say to others? Have your child describe to you what he is doing as he takes on the other role.

Having Fun With Language: Riddles

Knock, Knock.—*Who's there?*

Duane.—*Duane who?*

Duane the bathtub. I'm dwowning!

When my friend, Jason, was 3, he loved knock-knock jokes and riddles. I doubt that he understood the humor behind them all, but he delighted in them nevertheless. He sat with me one day while we went through a riddle book. I asked the questions, Jason delivered the answers with terrific expression, and I laughed with genuine pleasure at each silly one.

Learning the seemingly simple, but really quite complex sequence involved in a knock-knock joke is a good language-memory activity for young children. Riddles—learning to ask and then answer them—are also excellent language exercises.

The reason why jokes and riddles are so enjoyable for children is that the response to them is usually laughter. Telling jokes and riddles creates a happy atmosphere. Supplying the answers, making people laugh, provides a child with a success experience, a reason to enjoy language, to have fun with words.

I would encourage you to try to teach your young child some or all of the following jokes and riddles. One a day may be plenty. Help him practice until he is ready to ask someone else. Then, encourage him to tell his joke to older siblings, relatives, neighbors, just about anyone who will listen. Repetition, of course, is very important. Learning the riddles will provide your child with a reason to feel good about memorizing words which have meaning. Older children will gain a new confidence with language because they begin to see double meanings.

 ## RIDDLE ACTIVITIES

If your child can read, let him ask you the jokes and riddles below; otherwise, teach him the riddles so he can "use" them on his own. Look in the library for riddle books. The pictures which accompany the riddles make them even more fun.

- **Where does a sheep get a haircut?**—*At the baa-baa shop.*
- **Why does a hummingbird hum?**—*Because he doesn't know the words.*
- **How do you keep a dog off the road?**—*Put him in a barking lot.*
- **What do you call a bull when it's sleeping?**—*A bulldozer.*
- **What do cows like to do on Saturday nights?**—*Go to the MOO-vies.*
- **When is a farmer mean?**—*When he pulls ears off the corn.*
- **What do you call a crate full of ducks?** *A box of quackers.*
- **What did the baby porcupine say to the cactus?**—*Is that you, Mama?*

Knock, knock.—*Who's there?*
Eileen.—*Eileen who?*
Eileen'd on the fence too hard and it broke!

Knock, knock.—*Who's there?*
Amos.—*Amos who?*
Amosquito just bit me!

Writing:
The First Words

In the same way that understanding a language comes before speaking it, learning to read comes before learning to write. A child must first recognize the letters of the alphabet and have grasped the concept that letters are put together to form words, before he has a reason to write them himself. (See chapter 6 for more on learning basic printing skills.)

Once your child is beginning to decipher words and can write the letters of the alphabet, he will be eager to use his new skills. The more reasons he sees for writing, the more he will want to write, and the faster his skills will develop.

Usually the first thing a child wants to write is his own name. You can also show him how to write the names of other family members, friends, and relatives. With your help in spelling, he can write the grocery list, or write a note to someone.

One of the best reasons to write is to put stories on paper. Where before you wrote down the stories your child dictated to you, now he can write the words to accompany his pictures. You may want to write the words down for him to copy, or he may simply want to ask you for help with spelling. When his reading skills improve, he will probably try writing by himself, in which case you may have to ask him to read the story to you, as it may be hard to decipher if the spelling is far from correct. *Do not correct his spelling or printing at this point! Supporting and encouraging his attempts to express himself are far more important.*

Post your child's stories on the refrigerator, encourage him to read them to others, and make a file or find a box in which to keep at least samples of his work. Remember to date each. Some time in the future, it will be interesting for your child to see his early writing and realize how much he's improved.

Writing: Using Organizers

A different type of early writing activity involves the *process of categorization*. It was described by Dr. Robert Pehrsson of Idaho State University, at a reading conference I attended one fall. Consider these five words:

BIRDS   PLANES   TRAINS   BEES   KITES

Of the five words above, which one doesn't fit with the others? Trains? Right, because all the other things named can fly, and trains can't. Things which are related in some way can be placed in the same category.

Pehrsson explained the value of dealing with verbs rather than nouns when working with a beginning writer. A table is simply "there," unmoving, while swimming means action, and action is easier and much more fun to relate to and think about.

I agree with Pehrsson's belief that having young children act out different verbs can be extremely instructive. With the verb "swim" for instance, you can ask your child to be not only a person swimming, but a fish, a frog, or a dog. Have him act out hopping, skipping, driving a car, rolling down a hill, riding a bicycle, laughing, giggling, cooking, eating, typing, anything! Make a game of it with several children. Put rhythmic music behind it, and the children can listen, decide what action it sounds like, and then act out the appropriate verb.

Another valuable activity is to discuss pictures which show action. Use pictures in books, the newspaper or magazines, and ask questions like, "What is happening in this picture?", "Why?", "What do you think is going to happen next?" Encourage your child to give you full sentence descriptions of the actions—past, present, future. Help him learn a variety of verbs, so that instead of always using "running," he can choose from other verbs like "racing," "jogging," "speeding," "galloping," and use that which most accurately describes what he wants to say.

When it comes to writing, young children can be taught to write short paragraphs as soon as they can easily print the letters of the alphabet. Using pictures and words with young children, or just words with those who can already read, you can make *organizers* like the one below.

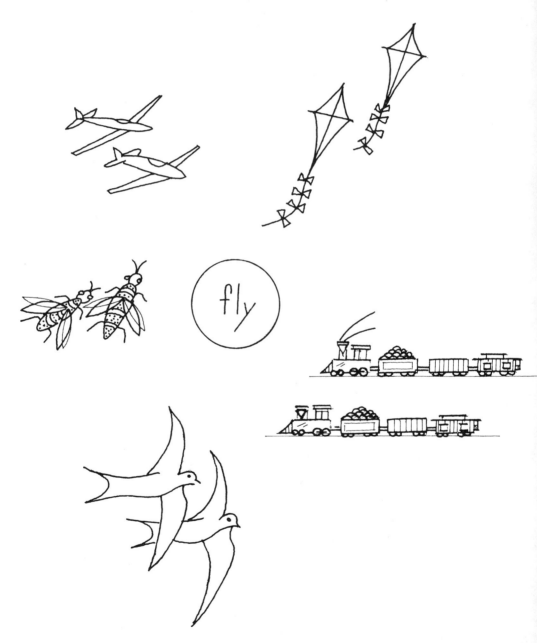

Pointing to the bees, ask your child to tell you what they are, and then ask whether or not they fly. When he says, "yes," ask him to draw a line connecting the bees with the central word "fly." Do the same with the other pictures. When you get to trains, and your child looks at you funny and says, "Trains don't fly!", have him draw a line to the word "fly," but then cross it to mean "don't." (Trains don't fly).

Once you have covered all the objects and decided which fly and which don't, you can help your child put this information into a short paragraph:

Planes fly. Kites fly. Birds fly. Bees fly. Trains don't fly.

Point out that it is helpful to group similar things together. In other words, tell all the things that do fly first, and then the one that doesn't.

Remember that it is easiest for a child to deal with verbs in the present tense and objects in the plural form. You avoid having to deal with "a, an, the." With even a very young child, you can point out the need for capitals and periods to "hold" his idea.

Putting Language to Use
Writing Thank-You Notes

Too often I read or hear about selfish young (and not so young) people who fail to even recognize receiving gifts from relatives who care enough to send them on special occasions. It embarrasses me. I have to agree with the often expressed thought that the culprit is not the child as much as the parent who did not teach his child this simple expression of thoughtfulness for others.

You aren't born knowing that you should think of others. You need to be taught, just as you are taught to tie your shoelaces. As a parent, you can help your child feel how important a simple thank-you note is to those relatives who could not share a special occasion in person, but whose thoughts were with him nonetheless. Help your child realize how important it is to think of others and how special those others are.

Even a child who cannot write by himself yet can dictate to you what he wants to say. He can draw a picture to go along with the note, or if he's able to, he can copy what you've written in his own printing, or proudly sign his name. It's up to you to teach him to give of himself.

A FEW MORE WRITING ACTIVITIES

➡ When you go for a walk with your child, have him take a small notepad and pencil with which to record events, things you see and hear. (For example: firetruck, flowers, dogs.) When you get back to the house, ask your child to help you write a short paragraph about your walk. Then encourage him to copy it.

➡ Encourage your child to make lists of:
- the foods he ate during the day
- colors
- animals
- friends, relatives
- sports, and so on.

MATH:
SO MUCH MORE
THAN COUNTING

From the time our son, Nathan, was a baby, I counted aloud a lot. I counted as I snapped up his clothes. I counted as I stacked blocks for him to knock down. I often held him on my left hip while I worked in the kitchen, counting "One, two, three," as I added cans of water to make orange juice.

One day when Nathan was a little over a year old, I stood by the kitchen sink, making juice, son on my hip. As I poured the first can of water, I said, "One." Before I could pour the second can, Nathan said, "Two." I thought perhaps he'd just made a sound that I wanted to believe was "two," but when he repeated the response—Mom was obviously pleased with it the first time!—I knew he was retrieving the word "two" from his memory. All my counting had not gone unnoticed!

With help from *Sesame Street*, Nathan, at 2 years, was counting pretty well and beginning to understand the concept involved.

Toddlers and preschoolers can and are happy to learn about numbers. They simply need someone to play number games with them. Introduce your child to the many ways in which you use numbers in your everyday life. Encourage him to use them. Expose him to basic geometric shapes, and help him become familiar with the simple concepts in math. If he feels comfortable with these, he will enjoy the challenge of dealing with more difficult concepts later on.

Most of us tend to concentrate our preschool "curriculum" at home on learning to read. We don't usually provide an equally rich opportunity for our youngsters to absorb numbers. It is important that we make an extra effort to offer lots of manipulative experiences. *Handling objects is extremely important for the development of a child's ability to think and learn in logical patterns.* In fact, in preschools and elementary schools, using manipulatives is the dominant approach to understanding math facts and concepts such as addition, subtraction, multiplication and division.

Introducing a Preschooler to Math Concepts

Parents are often thrilled to have friends and guests listen to their preschooler count to 10. That's OK. It is a chance for the child to show off, feel good about himself and learning.

But more than the ability to recite, what we want our children to have is a concept of what numbers are. For instance, if a child can't tell that there are three pencils on the table, or four people in the car, then knowing how to count obviously doesn't mean anything to him.

What you want to do is expose him to numbers and number concepts early, giving the numbers meaning. When you hand your child two crackers, say, "Here are two crackers. One," as he takes the first. "Two," as he takes the second. The more you use numbers, the sooner he will grasp the idea that each number corresponds to a certain amount.

The most valuable method of teaching a child number concepts is through the use of manipulatives. Give your child objects to play with, and ask questions which will encourage him to use the objects to find an answer. Provide him with opportunities to discover by himself, what numbers mean and how they can be used.

Sometime around the age of 4, or after he has begun writing letters, you can encourage your child to write numbers.

Math Concept Activities

❶ Be aware of opportunities to point out the meanings of: all vs. none, more vs. less, empty vs. full. Give your child cups to play with in the bathtub or sandbox to experiment with these concepts.

❷ Take advantage of the many opportunities to point out the different ways in which numbers are used: speed limit signs, address numbers, telephone numbers, speedometers, clocks, page numbers, and so on. Ask questions to help him learn to compare and understand relative sizes: "Which fish is bigger?" "Whose foot is larger?" "Whose hand is smaller?"

Other math vocabulary to introduce to your child: dozen, many, few, fewer, more, single, double, triple, bi-, tri-, uni-, mono-.

❸ Cut out cardboard "feet" (trace your child's!) and number then from 0 to 10. Arrange them in order and let your child walk on them, counting aloud as he goes.

❹ In the car, play counting games. You say "zero" and let him say "one." You then say "two" and let him say "three." And so on. Sometimes have him start the game and perhaps you can each say two numbers at a time. Ask questions like, "What number comes after three?" or "What number comes before seven?"

❺ Put some objects, like buttons, on the table. Move them around as if you're doing a magic trick, and then ask, "How many buttons are there?" Mix them up, removing or adding buttons, and ask again. Each time, help your child discover the correct answer by pointing to each button separately as you count them aloud. Then ask, "Can you count them?" Be sure he touches each as he counts aloud, so that he will see the one-to-one correspondence between number and object.

6 Consider purchasing a set of Cuisenaire Rods. (Check with a school supply store or write the Cuisenaire Co. for a brochure. See appendix.) Composed of wooden rods of different lengths and colors, they can help a child learn basic arithmetic concepts as well as how to add, subtract, multiply, and divide. Instructions for their use are included.

7 Encourage your child to watch *Sesame Street*, or better still, watch it with him. The program does a wonderful job of teaching the numbers 1–10.

8 Give your child a set of objects and ask him to arrange them from biggest to smallest and vice versa.

9 To help your child learn to recognize patterns:
• arrange popsicle sticks (which your child has helped you paint) into a pattern, such as "red-green-red-green." Ask your child to try and continue the pattern. This activity can be made more difficult by adding more colors, and increasing the length of the pattern to be repeated.
• Use an egg carton to create a pattern: a cotton ball in one cup, a button in the next, and so on.

10 Make a simple Bingo game and play with your child, where the goal can be to cover a row or the whole card.

3	7	1
9	4	8
5	2	6

11 Using a large piece of posterboard, make your own board game. Incorporate in the game, a topic of special interest to your child. For instance, if he likes playing with cars, draw a road or racetrack, and divide it into segments large enough to use small cars for "men." On some segments, write instructions like: "Go ahead 3 spaces" or "Go back 1 space." Use dice to determine moves. If your child has never played a board game before, *Candyland* is a good one to begin with. It uses pictures rather than numbers, but it is good for learning the process of game playing.

12 Play dice games like *Parcheesi* which require your child to count and move. *Sorry* is also a good board game using numbers. These games also introduce the concept of adding.

13 On blank index cards, write the numbers from 0 to 10, in words as well as numerals. Give your child a pile of paper clips and ask him to attach the corresponding number of clips to each card.

14 Give your child several different size jars or containers and some golf balls, walnuts, or ping pong balls. Ask him to guess how many it will take to fill each container. (The reason you want to use objects about the size of golf balls is that you don't want the containers to hold more than the child can count.)

15 Glue felt pieces onto 10 pieces of posterboard to create trees. On the trunk of each, glue a felt number (1–10). Cut 55 (maybe a few extra, just in case some get lost) small red apples out of felt. Ask your child to place the same number of apples on each tree as is written on the trunk.

16 Using a screwdriver, punch slits in the tops of 10 small baby food jars, big enough for pennies to fit easily through. Tape numbers from 1 to 10 on the sides of the jars. Give your child a supply of pennies and ask him to put coins in each jar to match the numbers on the sides.

17 If you have 10 small (matchbox-size) cars, make little "garages" for them. On the top of each garage, draw dots to illustrate a number from 1 to 10. On the roof of each car, tape a different number. Have your child drive each car into the "correct" garage, matching dots and numbers.

18 Cut up the front panel of your child's favorite cereal box and cut it into two puzzle pieces. Let him put the puzzle back together. If he has no trouble with that, cut the two pieces to make four. When he feels confident of putting the four pieces back together, cut them into more pieces for as long as the interest lasts. Be sure to stop before the puzzle becomes too frustrating. Keep it fun and positive!

19 Collect all your old buttons and let your child play with them. ("Hey, look what I found! I wonder what you could do with them.") Then watch to see what he does with them on his own. He will probably group them in some way. You can ask him also to group them in other ways—by size, by shape, by the number of holes in them, or by color. He will learn to look at one set of objects in several different ways, and classify them by attributes, though he won't know that's what he's doing!

20 Try Piaget's experiment on conservation of quantity. Find two identical juice glasses and a third glass which is taller and thinner than the other two. Fill the two juice glasses with equal amounts of juice. Place them in front of your child and ask, "Do both glasses have the same amount of juice?" Then pour the contents of one of the glasses into the tall, thin glass and ask, "Does one of the glasses have more juice than the other?" If he answers that the thin glass has more juice, ask why he thinks so. Then pour the juice back into the juice glass and ask again. Don't use this playtime to try to explain why he is wrong. Until he figures out the concept involved *for himself*, he won't understand it. *Your role at this point is to set up the learning situation and encourage experimentation so that your child can discover new ideas on his own.* You can also try pouring the juice into a shallow dish to see what your child thinks.

21 Using 3 or 4 different colors of posterboard, cut up squares, circles, and triangles, at least 2 of each. Review the shapes and colors with your child. Ask him to group the squares (or circles or triangles) by color. Try giving your child all the red shapes; ask him to group them by shape. Create a pattern and have your child copy it. (For example: red square, blue circle, yellow triangle, green triangle.) You'll think of more ideas as you and your child play with the shapes.

Addition and Subtraction

Learning to add and subtract will be most easily accomplished if a child has *reason* to perform these operations. If you can teach the concepts through *play*, they will be learned more easily and quickly.

As with reading, *you don't want to push* a child; simply encourage by providing opportunities to discover the concepts, and practice the operations.

ADDITION AND SUBTRACTION ACTIVITIES

➡ If your child seems intrigued by numbers and the idea of adding, you can make flash cards. Be sure that using them is fun. Flip through the cards quickly and play for a short time only. Encourage your child to say the whole fact, and not just the answer. This adds the dimension of hearing, which is how some children learn best. When your child gives an incorrect answer, simply supply the correct one and go on. Return to the card later and try again. You can use large index cards to make traditional flash cards. For fun sometimes, let your child quiz you! He'll enjoy switching roles, and he'll still get the practice.

FRONT

$$3 \\ +2$$

BACK

$$3 \\ +2 \\ \hline 5$$

FRONT

$$3+2=$$

BACK

$$3+2=5$$

➡️ It is valuable for your child to learn that math facts form "families." There are 4 facts in each—2 addition and 2 subtraction. In each fact, the numbers are the same. Only the order and operation are different. For instance, 3, 2, and 5 make the following four facts:

$$3+2=5 \qquad 2+3=5 \qquad 5-2=3 \qquad 5-3=2$$

A variation of the traditional flash card can be introduced to present the three numbers of the fact together. Hold up each card and ask your child to supply the four facts involved. At first you might want to point to the numbers to help as he says them.

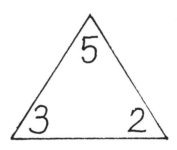

➡️ Make and play board games like *Parcheesi*, where two dice are used. Adding the numbers will happen automatically after a while. After rolling "2" and "3" enough times, and hearing you say "5" as he moves his player, it won't be long before he thinks "5" when he rolls a "2" and a "3."

➡️ Make a large number line (0–10) on the floor or in chalk on the driveway (it will wash away), and have your child stand on any number he chooses. Ask him to move ahead 4 spaces and tell you where he is. Simply state the fact involved ("3" plus "4" equals "7").

➡️ Make a game of *Concentration*, where one card in the pair has the problem, and the other card has the answer. Make 5 or 6 pairs and scatter them face down on the rug or table. Take turns turning over two cards and trying to locate two that belong together. (This is a good memory exercise, too!)

Time

With digital clocks and watches everywhere, some of the pressure to learn to tell time has decreased, but not much. It is still an important skill for your child to learn. Besides, there is much more to understanding time than reading a clock.

With a preschooler, you can introduce time-related vocabulary such as morning, afternoon, evening, night, tomorrow, today and yesterday. Explain the terms in words your child will understand. For instance, "This afternoon, we're going to the library. We'll go after lunch, in the afternoon." It may sound repetitious to you, but it will help your child understand that "in the afternoon" means sometime after lunch.

Ask your preschooler questions like, "Can you tell Grandma what you did this morning?" "Where are we going tomorrow?" "Who did we visit yesterday?"

The best way to teach someone how to tell time is to get a clock with a second hand and play around with it. Depending on your child's age, arrange the hands at times he should be able to recognize. With a preschooler, you may find it helpful to teach your child that when the clock says 1:00, it is time for a nap, or that 8:00 means bedtime. He may want to know when *Sesame Street* comes on television. Concrete uses of a clock will give a child a reason to learn to tell time.

Money

You can introduce a preschooler to money by simply pointing out the different coins we use. Encourage him to notice which one is the biggest, which is the smallest, which one is brown. Point out the different markings and help him learn the correct names for each coin. When he is ready, explain that each coin has a different value.

When you are paying for groceries or a hamburger and french fries at a fast food restaurant, explain to your child the idea that you are trading money for the food. When you're not in a hurry, let him pay for a particular item, handing the money to the cashier and receiving any change. Encourage your child to play "store" at home. Make or buy him a piggy bank and introduce the idea of saving.

Geometry

How can you recognize a STOP sign or a YIELD sign when you can see only the back of it? By its shape, just as you can tell time on a clock with no numbers by the angle of its two hands. If you stop and look around the room in which you are sitting, you become aware of the shapes which make up your environment. The picture on the wall is a rectangle. The knob on the door is a circle. The cord on the telephone is a spiral and so on.

You can help a preschooler to develop a solid foundation in geometry by introducing him to the basic shapes in the world around him: circle, square, triangle, and rectangle.

Find objects for your child to trace (he may need help learning to trace) which will result in the shapes he's learned. For example, a coin or a margarine container lid will make a circle, books will make rectangles. If you look around your house you will find lots of objects to use, though you may have to use your imagination more for the triangle. A sandwich cut in half diagonally would provide a triangle, but might be messy for tracing! It's fun to draw lots of shapes on construction paper and color them in with designs and bright colored markers, giving some eyes, or whiskers, or hats. Children can really get into this kind of creative play with shapes. You may even end up with a masterpiece to frame!

Use blank index cards to make flash cards of these shapes for review in a free moment. Make it a game, keep it fast and fun. When opportunities arise to introduce other shapes, take advantage of them. Look at the moon from time to time and introduce the word *crescent*. You can explain that a stop sign has six sides and is called a *hexagon*. Add three-dimensional shapes, too: a block is called a *cube*, an ice cream *cone*, a ball is a *sphere*, a can is a *cylinder*, and so on.

If you work with your child on these concepts and try the following activities, he will start noticing the shapes of everything within a very short time. The nice thing about shapes is that they are literally everywhere, in the grocery store, on the dashboard of the car, in the backyard, on your body. Discover with your child, all the shapes which make up the world. Encourage him to try drawing them, and help him create three-dimensional shapes from clay or paper. In doing so, you will both become more observant and aware of all the shapes around you, and how they are used.

GEOMETRY ACTIVITIES

➡ Make three "4 × 4" squares of posterboard. Leave one whole, and cut the other two as follows:

On larger pieces of paper or posterboard, draw shapes like those below and ask your child to cover them exactly, using the square and four halves you cut.

Encourage your child to play with the pieces to create a house, a sailboat, etc.

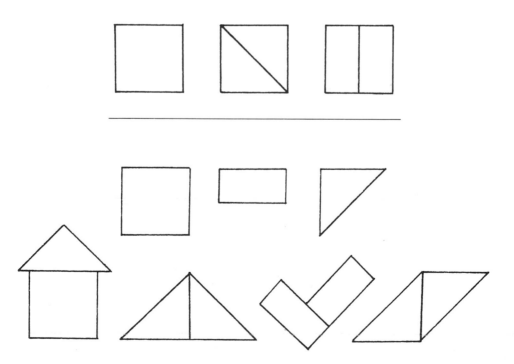

THREE-DIMENSIONAL SHAPE ACTIVITIES

➡ Play with cubes. Help your child stick a cut-out picture on each face of a cube. (A square wooden block will work.) Ask him questions such as, "How many pictures can you see from where you are?" "Which picture can nobody see?"

➡ Use touch as well as sight. Encourage your child to feel along the edges and the sides of a cube. How many of each are there? Introduce the terms and the concepts:

A cube has 6 *faces* and 8 *corners*.
The shape of each face is a *square*.
Two faces meet at an *edge*.

➡ Discuss the concept "surface" (of a pond, a table, a ball), and the fact that some are flat and some are curved. Let your child hold and describe the surfaces of different objects such as a book, a can, or a tennis ball. Introduce the terms *cylinder* and *sphere* and discuss the characteristics of each.

➡ Help your child trace around different objects to learn the shapes their outlines make. Let him color inside the outlines to create a design! Once he understands the idea, ask him what shape he would get if he traced around a plate, a toothpaste carton, etc.

Fun With Graphs

Visual aids are commonly used to illustrate facts and figures. We see charts and graphs in the newspaper, in magazines, and on television. A preschooler will enjoy making graphs to explain the results of a simple experiment or poll. In the process, he will practice the fundamental thinking skills involved in categorizing and counting. Below are three graphs you can help your child construct. Encourage him to think of more.

GRAPHING ACTIVITIES

➡ A Taste Test: Have your child choose three types of juice and offer samples to members of the family and/or neighbors, friends, and relatives. He should ask each person to tell which he liked most. Help him show the results on a graph with smiley faces. When finished, add up the faces in each column and write the totals at the bottom.

A TASTE TEST		
apple	grape	orange
☺ ☺	☺	☺ ☺ ☺
2	1	3

➡ Graph the results of a scientific experiment. For instance, find 6 or 8 objects to test as to whether or not they will rust if placed in water. Objects might include a paper clip, a crayon, an eraser, a nail, and so on.

Have your child draw a picture of each object (you may have to help him) under the correct column.

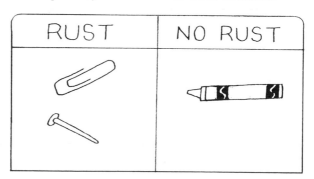

RUST	NO RUST

➡ Make a graph to show what color is the favorite.
Put a star in a box for each vote.

Favorite Colors						
red	☆	☆	☆	☆		
blue	☆	☆	☆	☆	☆	
green	☆					
yellow	☆	☆	☆			
purple	☆	☆				
pink	☆	☆				
black	☆					
white						
other	☆					

DEVELOPING
MUSCLES,
COORDINATION,
AND "GOOD SPORTS"

Outdoor Play

Bill was bent over, pushing a toy lawnmower. Beside him, his 1½-year-old daughter, Becky, pushed her child-size wheelbarrow. They talked and laughed as they often do, playing together in their backyard. This is just one of many father-daughter scenes I have witnessed from our kitchen window as I've stood there, washing what seems to be an endless pile of dirty dishes.

One Saturday not long ago, Bill was busy with his power saw, cutting into the ends of some long wooden posts. Curiosity finally got the better of me, and I asked, over the back fence, what he was building. "A sandbox," he replied.

A few days later, when it was finished and filled with sand, I took a closer look. I could see then how Bill had cut away half of each log end, to fit them together. It's a beautiful, large sandbox, one I'm sure Becky (and Bill) will enjoy for years.

As the weather turns warmer, we tend to spend more time outdoors, encouraging our children to do the same. I encourage you to do what you can to provide some play equipment in your yard, to help your child develop his motor skills, and engage in fantasy and investigative play, as Becky is now able to do in her sandbox.

In *Learning For Little Kids*, author Sandy Jones offers the following ideas for making play equipment from scrounged things:

✔ Ropes, rope ladders, and cargo nets from hardware stores and shipyards, for climbing and swinging.

✔ Barrels, from a hardware store or a distillery, for rolling in, making houses and tunnels. (Be sure to sand away the splinters.)

✔ A discarded rowboat (ask around piers and docks); use for imaginary voyages, or drill holes for drainage and use for a sandbox.

✔ An old washtub, sunken in the ground, for water play.

✔ Tree sections and tree trunks with limbs, from city electric company, neighbors or a lumber mill; for climbing, and practicing hammering and sawing.

✔ A sawhorse, to cover for a tent.

✔ Wooden blocks and pieces of lumber, for building structures with hammer and nails, for stacking and other structures.

✔ An old wooden ladder to lay on the ground for part of an obstacle course.

✔ Old car and truck tires, from auto junkyards and service stations. Clean them up, paint them if you want with bright colors. They're extremely versatile.

TIRES

Swing Made with Rope

Obstacle Course

Tunnel

Spin-around Swing

Tire Cut in Half for Water Play

Ride'm Horsey Tire

A Suspended Climber
(tires are bolted together)

Outdoor Activities

➡ Draw pictures in the dirt with a stick.

➡ Float paper boats on puddles.

➡ Have a water balloon fight.

➡ Blow bubbles.

➡ Have wheelbarrow races.

➡ Take a blindman's walk: one person is blindfolded, the other leads him and presents objects for the blindfolded person to identify.

➡ Play games like "Simon Says," "Mother May I," "Red Light-Green Light," "Flashlight Tag," and "Hide-and-Seek."

➡ Play "Hopscotch."

➡ Find a park with hills to roll down.

➡ Play circus. Let your child crawl on top of you, and stand on your hands. Lie on your back and balance your child on your feet. Do cartwheels, handstands, somersaults.

➡ Pick wildflowers or autumn leaves. Take them home and look them up in a nature book. (*Peterson's Field Guides* are perfect for children, too.) Press the flowers or leaves and label, or paste them in a homemade nature book.

➡ Skip stones across water.

➡ Play in puddles after a summer rain.

➡ Work in the garden together.

Developing Specific Body Skills

"Many parents encourage their children's learning by providing them with books, crayons, paints, and other learning materials while neglecting the all-important business of helping them master their bodies."

The above is a somewhat eye-opening observation made by Raymond Stinar in his article, "Helping Your Child to Develop Body Skills." Unfortunately, the comment is all too close to the truth. Stinar describes another part of the problem when he tells the following story:

> *"People around the pool would watch my children swimming and would ask me if I would teach their children to swim. I would always reply that 'all you have to do is get out of your lounge chair, get into the water and play with your child,' but no one seemed to want to take the trouble to become involved with their children."*

The early years are critical in motor development. Though the quality of performance continues to improve, no new basic body skills appear in a child's movement repertoire after the age of five or six. That's why it is so important that parents take an active role in teaching their young children these basic motor skills.

Below are some of the skills Stinar suggests you do together with your child. Stinar asks, and I wholeheartedly agree, that you follow two simple rules when doing these activities:

❶ Don't force your child to do anything he doesn't want to.

❷ Don't be concerned about the quality of your child's performance.

There should be no pressure or feeling of competition. Along with developing your child's body skills, your main goal is to have fun.

Basic Body Skill Activities

THROWING AND CATCHING BALLS

Throwing. Ideally, you should begin these activities with balls which fit easily into the hand, like a tennis ball.

Catching. Roll the ball to your child to catch. Roll it to his right and left, and then while he's moving. Show your child how to bounce the ball to himself and catch it. Once he's comfortable with that, have him toss the ball in the air and catch it after it bounced once or twice or three times. Bounce a ball to him or toss it to him in an arc. Lastly, help your child practice catching while he's on the move.

 ➡ Have your child begin by throwing the ball while he stands still. Next ask him to throw it as far as he can. Have him try throwing it overhand, underhand and sidearm. Show him how to throw at large targets (a wall, a fence), and gradually aim at smaller targets. Finally, have him throw any of these ways, while moving.

➡ Make a scoop from an old bleach bottle. Have your child try catching with it, first while standing still, then while moving. Then have him try catching with a baseball glove.

HITTING A BALL

 ➡ Begin with large, slow balls (beach balls, balloons, foam balls) and change gradually to smaller, faster balls.

➡ Ask your child to try hitting a non-moving ball with his fist, elbow, foot, or other part of his body.

➡ Have him hit the ball hard, then softly. Ask him to try and hit the ball and make it go up, down and to the side.

➡️ Once your child can hit a non-moving ball, encourage him to try hitting a moving ball, rolled or thrown to him by someone else.

BATTING A BALL

➡️ Start with a large surfaced paddle. Move on to rackets and then fat plastic toy bats. Begin with large balls, and progress to smaller balls of different materials.

➡️ Have your child strike the ball first while it is not moving, then while it's rolling. Next encourage him to try hitting a bouncing ball. Finally, help him hit a ball tossed by you or one that he tosses in the air himself.

DRIBBLING A BALL

➡️ Starting with a large ball, help your child bounce it with two hands. Explain that he's not supposed to catch the ball, but instead, hit it while he is standing still. Once he has the idea, ask him to try bouncing the ball with one hand, then the other. Finally show him how to bounce the ball while moving around.

➡️ Show your child that a ball can also be moved around by kicking it with different parts of one's feet— toes, heels, inside or outside of the foot.

BALANCING

➡️ Ask your child to balance on tiptoe with his arms at his side. Next have him try it with arms overhead. Show him how to stretch way up and squat down low. Have him try balancing on one foot; with eyes closed; with arms up, down, and out to the side.

➡️ Help your child balance on his hands with his feet over his head, knees resting on his elbows.

➡ Help him balance on his hands while you hold his feet.

➡ Make a balance beam, and coffee canrope stilts for your child to play on.

LEARNING HOW TO MOVE AND RUN

➡ Ask your child to walk forward, backward, and sideways. Next have him run in these different directions. Play a game where he runs and changes direction when you tell him to. Play tag.

➡ Have your child try jumping on one foot and both feet. Next have him try leaping and landing on both feet (running long jump). Set up small obstacles for him to jump over. Show him how to jump for distance by standing on both feet, swinging his arms to help with momentum, and landing on both feet.

➡ Demonstrate skipping and galloping (one foot always leading).

➡ Help your child roll in a somersault. Ask him to roll like a log, with his arms by his side or over his head. Have him try rolling slowly, quickly, forward, backward, down a hill, and up a hill.

HANGING, SWINGING, AND CLIMBING

➡ Encourage your child to find as many ways as he can to climb up and down a jungle gym, bar, or tree limb. Help him hang by his hands, knees, both. Ask him to swing in different ways.

Parents, do some "roughhousing" on the floor with your child. Roll around together, let your child crawl on you, hang on you, balance on you. Have a mock wrestling match where your child tries to pin you down. Keep it fun with lots of exaggerated gasps and terror!

Body Awareness

The following "body awareness" activities will allow you to increase your child's degree of awareness of his own body and its capabilities in movement. Children who are confident about their bodies are generally more confident overall. They also tend to "know their own strength" and as a result can be physically athletic, and gentle too.

 ❶ Identifying body parts. Here's my head. Touch your head. (elbow, ear, knee, and so on). Can you touch your head with your hand? your left elbow to your right knee?

❷ Movement. Instruct your child to: run fast; run slowly; run fast, slow down, and run fast again. How slowly can you move? How fast can you move your arms in a circle? Have your child run (skip, walk) keeping time to a drum beat.

❸ Strength and force. Can you move softly? like a feather? Now move strongly and make lots of noise with your feet. Be a floppy rag doll; now be a tight spring.

❹ Body shape. Make yourself long and narrow; make yourself big and wide. Curl into the tiniest ball you can. Change from a ball to a bat. With your body, make the letters of your name, or the alphabet, or make the number 2 (5, 6, 7, or 9).

❺ Walking movements. Walk forward, sideward, backward, zig-zag, on tiptoes, on your heels, with knees high, with toes in, with toes out, as if in a parade.

❻ Running movements. Run in place; run fast, slow, around objects; run and jump; run and stop on signal and run again; run following a leader.

❼ Leaping and jumping. Jump over a rope on the floor. Jump across a distance between two ropes on the floor (increase the distance a little each time). Jump over small obstacles.

---

8 Draw stick figures and ask your child to copy them with his own body. (Doing it in front of a mirror might help.) Some figures require a partner.

Sportsmanship, Competition, Cooperation

Scotty, a straight A student, voted by his classmates as the class leader, was waiting for the kickball pitch. The ball bounced gently toward Scotty, he kicked wildly, completely missed the ball, and landed on his seat in the dirt.

Once I saw that he was all right, I smiled, and then chuckled. Scotty picked himself up, shook his head, and laughed at his blunder. Right there in front of all his peers, he'd done what we all would tend to agree is rather embarrassing. But Scotty had the self-confidence to laugh at his mistake, be a good sport, and continue with the game. He was not angry, and the world had not come to an end. What a great role model for his peers!

The attitudes teachers see in Physical Education at school reflect the attitudes that children have learned at home concerning competition and sportsmanship. How children approach team sports, as well as academics, or any potentially competitive situation, depends on the sort of guidelines their parents have put down, and the example they have set.

Children, simply because they are children, enjoy playing. It may be hard for some adults to believe or understand, but children are usually not terribly worried about who wins or loses, but are concerned with having fun. It is we adults who bring the idea of competition and winning into their lives.

I am concerned about children who are preoccupied with winning, who get really angry when they lose a game. At the same time, I believe that competition is not all bad, especially when it involves setting goals for oneself. There is value in competing against oneself, striving always to do better, whether in academics, in playing a musical instrument, or in sports. Competition can lead to a development of interest in one's own progress as an individual.

There is nothing wrong in wanting to win a baseball game, either, as long as your child remembers that that's what it is—a game. Encourage him to enjoy it while he plays. He should try to win because he should always try to do his best, but he should also know how to win or lose gracefully, and put the game behind him once it's over. The spirit of competition has as much to do with the fun of playing, as it does with rivalry and the desire to win. Children clearly take their cues from their parents on this.

As a parent, consider yourself the key role model. Stop and ask yourself what kind of example you are setting when you find yourself in a competitive situation. If, upon losing a tennis match or a card game, you grumble about the other player cheating, or you make excuses for your own failure to win, you present an example of poor sportsmanship to your child.

If, however, you can respond to competitive situations in a positive way, and let your child see that such experiences can be chances to learn and grow, not to mention simply have fun, then you will do him a great favor.

You can best help your child deal with competition and the feelings involved if you are there when the competition is over. At that point, you can turn the situation into a learning experience. If your child has won, let him feel good and be proud of himself, but not to the point of offending the losers. In that case, it's pretty fair to say to anyone that no matter how good he is, there's always someone better. Teach your child to be a humble winner.

If your child lost, give him a hug or an arm around the shoulder. Let him know that you're proud of him because you know he tried, and that's what matters. All anyone can ask of another is that he do his best. When the time is right (after a cooling-off period), you can discuss with your child why he feels he or his team lost. If you sense he feels a weakness in his own abilities, or if he expresses a desire to improve his skills, offer to help. Reinforce the idea that if he's learned something (even if it's what he needs to work on), then he's gained from the experience, and he is a winner, too.

Some children honestly won't care if they won or lost. They are simply thrilled to be a part of a team. That's certainly fine!

Even if you cannot be at your child's games, you can still help him deal with competition and the feelings that accompany winning and losing. Most of all, you can teach him to keep things in perspective. When he comes home from a game, ask him, "Did you have fun?", rather than, "Did you win?" By not focusing on winning or losing, you can help your child see that there are more important things.

As we must help our children put competition in perspective, we need to do the same ourselves. I hear stories about Little League and similar organized sports, where the adults in charge take everything so seriously. Some don't let all the team members play. Only the best-skilled play so that the team has a better chance of winning. To me, if you don't use all of your players, it's not a real team, and the whole point of the sport at this level is missed. What is more important: to have a winning team with half of its players never leaving the bench, their self-esteem decreasing a little more each game, or a "losing" team where all the players get to play, and win or lose, they're all made to feel they've tried hard, done their best? There is no doubt in my mind which is the more valuable goal.

The other side of the coin in this matter is cooperation. To me this is the more valuable of the two characteristics to encourage. When you come right down to it, far less would be accomplished in this world if we were all constantly competing, instead of cooperating.

When children organize a game of some sort, they inevitably have disputes and problems. How tempting to an adult nearby to break in and try to straighten things out, set down rules. We need to refrain from this whenever possible. *Children learn a lot by having to work out their problems and settle their disputes among themselves.* They learn to compromise and to get along.

Before a child learns to cooperate with others, he needs to develop an awareness of the people in the world around him. You can help by drawing your child's attention to others, first simply to their physical presence, then to their emotional state. Ask your child questions which will encourage him to consider how others feel in various situations. "Why do you think that boy is crying?" "How would you feel if that happened to you?"

Make an effort to provide situations in which your child is rewarded by cooperating with another person. As it's usually easier for him to cooperate with an adult, start by providing him with opportunities to help you. For instance, invite your child to play a game with you after you put the dishes in the dishwasher. Mention that if he'd like to help, you'd be able to play sooner. Then you might hand him the dishes to put in the machine.

As siblings often find cooperation difficult, you can provide situations in which it's to their benefit to cooperate. For example, offer to take them swimming if they'll work together to put the trash out or pick up the family room.

You can further encourage cooperation between siblings by sharing a secret with them about something special. A feeling of closeness and camaraderie tends to develop among people who share a secret. Your guidance and encouragement is always advised! "Gee, I'm really proud of you two! You're doing a great job together!" Some tasks you might set out for siblings or peer groups to do together include working on a jigsaw puzzle, making ice cream, raking leaves, painting a mural on a wall, and working on a creative project together.

Help your child see the value of both competition and cooperation. Help him to be a good sport, and show him how to deal with winning and losing. Be aware of the example you set. Finally, don't let yourself be one of those who say, "Do as I say, not as I do." We all know which is the more effective teacher.

CREATIVE THINKING

Brainstorming

Suppose someone handed you a small tree to plant this fall, saying that it would grow to six times its present size by spring. Not only this, but it will grow anything you choose on its branches. Toss the thought about for a few minutes with your family. What kind of tree would you want or could it be? One that grows money, or hugs, or chocolate chip cookies? One little boy reportedly described a tree that, when given his homework after school, would have it completed and ready for him the next morning!

When you sit down and toss around as many possible solutions to a problem as you can think of, you are *brainstorming*. Brainstorming is important because it is the first step in the process of creative problem solving. Creative solutions involve: *fluency* (generating lots of ideas), *flexibility* (accepting the possibility of more than one answer to a problem, more than one use for an object), *originality* (creating ideas which are unusual, different), and *elaboration* (taking an idea "one step further").

As parents, you can do much to foster creativity in your children. Try to encourage divergent thinking, unusual ideas. Allow your child to experiment with ideas without criticism. The creative thinking process helps children develop abilities to deal with problems and new situations he encounters.

Rides in the car, meals, bedtime, or any time you set aside to spend with your child, are great times to begin encouraging creative thinking. You will awaken part of your child's brain that can prove to be a useful and enjoyable tool. Instead of performing tasks in the usual, prescribed manner, he will learn to invent alternative methods. A child who sees the advantage to flexibility, won't be so apt to resist new concepts in math when he encounters them. He will be willing to consider alternatives in his attempts to solve problems in science, and his stories and creative writing skills are likely to improve dramatically.

A person with the ability to think creatively has more control over his own life, more power to influence the lives of others with inventions or solutions to practical problems or emergency situations. Help your child gain that extra control over his own life, and expand his mind to see more than he might otherwise see.

Creative Thinking Activities

➡ Help your child become aware of his senses. When you take a walk, encourage him to not only look at things, but touch, smell, and listen whenever practical. Introduce him to different textures, and discuss how they feel. Close your eyes sometimes and listen to and identify as many sounds as you can.

➡ When your child uses a book to make a tunnel for his cars, or makes a house from a large carton, show some excitement ("What a neat idea!") and encourage his creativity.

➡ Encourage your child to make presents for people, ornaments for your Christmas tree, his own Halloween costume.

➡ Instead of throwing away old boxes and containers, find and encourage others in your family to also find new uses for them.

➡ Ask a lot of "What if . . ." type questions. Example: "What if you went camping and forgot your toothbrush? Can you come up with other ways to brush your teeth?"

➡️ Keep a "scrounge box" filled with scraps of fabric, wood, paper towel tubes, shoe boxes, ribbons, egg cartons, coffee cans, left-over wallpaper—just about anything you can think of. Invite your child to make new inventions, decorative items, gifts, or whatever he'd like. This is especially nice to have on a long, rainy day.

➡ Pretend you suddenly find yourself in a difficult situation. Your child can help you imagine something specific. Try to think of all the good or positive things you can find in that situation. Encourage your child to look for possible solutions, ways in which he could get himself out of that same situation.

➡ Brainstorm about anything! What uses could you find for a styrofoam cup besides drinking? For a fork besides eating? For a piece of paper besides writing? For a nickel besides spending as money? If it were to rain on the day you'd planned to have a picnic, what else could you do to have fun?

Roadblocking

"What would you do if you got home and found yourself locked out of the house?"

"I'd bang on the door to see if anyone was in there to let me in."

"O.K., but what do you do when no one comes?"

"Look for the spare key under the doormat."

"Ah, but your sister used it last night to come in from her late date and then left it inside."

"Then I'd look around the house for an open window."

"Good idea, but it poured rain last night and your mother shut and locked all the windows in the house."

"I could break the window in the door and reach inside and unlock the door."

"But your father just installed an alarm system and if you broke a window, the police would come."

"Then I'd go to the neighbor's to wait until someone else got home and let me in."

"But your neighbors left yesterday for a vacation in Hawaii."

Is the above conversation beginning to drive you crazy in an "Oh, brother!" sort of way? It is an attempt to illustrate what Dr. Rick Neel (Professor of Education, University of Washington) called *roadblocking*.

Roadblocking begins with giving the child a hypothetical situation like the one above, and asking him how he would deal with it. You, in turn, come up with a reason why that particular solution won't work, forcing the child to think of an alternative. Your roadblocks can be crazy and funny. The point is simply to keep your child searching for more possible solutions. For fun, sometimes let your child give you a problem and set up roadblocks for you to overcome.

If you spend a few minutes on this type of activity once in a while—in the car, at the dinner table, or while tucking your child in for the night—you will help him open his mind to considering lots of possible alternatives for dealing with problems. When he eventually runs into similar situations, he will be used to looking for more than one answer. Children who learn to weave their way through roadblocks excel in many academic areas—science, language arts, social studies—because they are creative thinkers.

Roadblocking can be used with children as young as 4 or 5 to help them think of what to do if a problem arises and you're not there. It can be a valuable safety drill if you deal with a situation such as: "What would you do if we went to the store and you got lost and couldn't find me?"

ROADBLOCK ACTIVITIES

➡ What would you do if a little puppy started following you as you walked home from the store?

➡ You're filling up a small swimming pool in your backyard. When you go to turn off the water, it won't stop, even though you've turned the faucet all the way. What would you do?

➡ What would you do if suddenly you couldn't talk?

➡ What would you do if you were home alone and the lights went out?

➡ What would you do if your older brother who always let you play with him before, tells you one day to quit hanging around him anymore?

A TREASURE HUNT

Once or twice a year, I set up a treasure hunt for my students. One clue might simply read, "H_2O", directing each team in turn to check the water fountains for the next clue. This clue might be a riddle leading them to another classroom where one student from each team would have to spell a particularly difficult word they have been tested on in the past. A third clue might be a coded message, and so on. The treasure hunt continues until each team's last clue has directed the student back to me.

While a few competitive individuals seem frustrated when they discover they haven't "won," the overwhelming majority of the students return from the treasure hunt literally flushed with excitement. The enthusiasm on their faces makes the effort I've put into the planning, well worth it. I have sparked their brains with the challenge of riddles and puzzles, forcing them to think creatively, to look beyond the obvious.

Weekends, summer, birthday parties, or a holiday vacation would be a great time to set up a treasure hunt for your children, or child and friends. For a younger child you will probably want to keep it to your own house. Below are some ideas for clues for a beginning treasure hunter:

 1 Draw or cut out pictures of things to direct your child from one clue to another. (Examples: a box of cereal, a cookie jar, the bathtub or sink, his bed, a chair, the television, the telephone, the refrigerator, the mailbox, or a bicycle.)

2 With a primary-age child, you might try simple riddles like, "Bugs Bunny eats me," to lead him to the carrots in the refrigerator; "I tell you what time it is," for a clock; "You can talk to your friends with me even when you can't see them," for a telephone, and so on.

The possibilities are endless. The setting-up requires a little thought and organization, but not an overwhelming amount of time. If you plan a hunt for a single child or team, it's not hard at all. With two teams, make two sets of identical clues. Just arrange them in differen orders, with the last clue for each team leading back to you.

The "treasure" can be anything—hot chocolate and cookies, an invitation to your child's best friend or friends to spend the night, a movie, a comic book, a deck of cards, anything!

OTHER ACTIVITIES
TO FOSTER CREATIVITY

 ➡ Do some role playing. Have your child act out the roles of those involved in different careers.

➡ Listen creatively to music (instrumental, classical, jazz, and so on) and let the sound stimulate a flow from one thought to another. Listen together to a piece of music, eyes closed, and afterwards share the different images and thoughts and feelings you experienced.

➡ Construct puppets and give plays.

➡ Work on jigsaw puzzles. Start with simple puzzles. You can even make your own by cutting up the front of a cereal box, or by gluing a picture your child made, onto a piece of cardboard and cutting it into pieces.

➡ Keep a "costume box" filled with fun clothes, shoes, hats, nightgowns, jewelry, ties, feathers, scarves. Encourage children to play dress-up and then create impromptu skits with their characters. For older children, encourage role-playing by suggesting characters and situations for them to dress up and act out.

➡ Give children some basic ingredients and have them make a special salad or luncheon platter. Have them "name" their creation.

➡ Put on a variety show—magic, song and dance, skits, gymnastics. Invite neighbors and serve lemonade and cookies.

CHAPTER

11

ENCOURAGING YOUR CHILD'S CURIOSITY

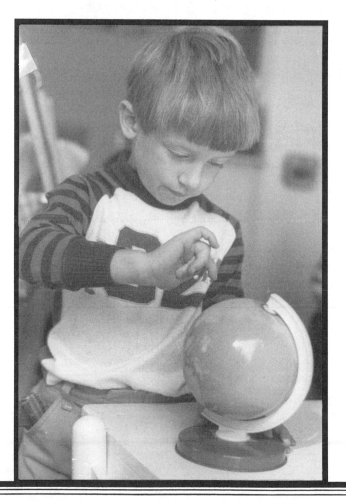

When I knew Steven, he was a 12-year-old with unending curiosity. He would spend literally hours playing in his room, creating working replicas of machines, as well as inventions of his own from cardboard and odds and ends he'd saved or salvaged from what others had discarded. Steven also enjoyed digging in the earth, discovering and observing the creatures that live there. He made bird feeders, a terrarium, and pressed flowers he had picked to make cards for people. He observed and appreciated the world around him. He questioned how things work and searched for answers. He tested his own theories.

Unfortunately, too many children seem to possess less curiosity and ask fewer questions than Steven did. They lack the know-how or desire to search for answers on their own.

Science is a subject with which many of us feel uncomfortable. The word by itself creates images of laboratories, experiments, complicated theories, chemicals, an endless and incomprehensible universe.

But the truth of the matter is that all of us know and can teach far more science than we realize. We use and deal with countless machines and concepts of science each day! We can all work to help children develop more interest in science and thus more confidence in their ability to deal with things scientific.

We can encourage a child to question, observe, describe, measure, and test.

Question. With a young child, begin by posing questions yourself. "I wonder why this plant is dropping leaves?" "What do you suppose that bird is going to do with that piece of string?" "Where did my shadow go?" Offer possible answers, and ask your child what he thinks. Remember, children love to imitate. If your child sees you looking around, noticing things and asking questions, he will follow suit.

Observe. Children tend to want to get up close and touch things, so simply observing is a difficult skill to learn. And yet, even a 3-year-old can learn to be very quiet and still. For instance, when they spot a rabbit in the wild, most youngsters will immediately want to touch it. In their excitement, they run toward it, and the rabbit quickly hops away. After a few such incidents, a child can usually be convinced to be still, so that he can watch the animal.

The next time the two of you spot a rabbit, or any animal, squat down beside your child, put your arm around him, and whisper in his ear things for him to observe. Make it a game, a special secret you're sharing. "Look at his whiskers." "Do you see him wiggling his nose?" "What does his tail look like?" When you return home, make a point of encouraging your child to describe to other family members what he saw.

In addition to watching birds, animals, and insects, a child can learn to observe changes in the sky, the clouds, the moon, the trees, and so on.

Describe. An important part of science (and communication) is learning to describe things. You can help your child become aware of the many characteristics of an object by asking him questions. "What color is that rock?" "Is it heavy or light?" "What does it feel like?" "Is it warm or cold?" "Why?" "What shape is the rock?"

Measure. While making exact measurements in inches, feet, yards, ounces, pounds, and so on, is a skill a young child can't be expected to learn, a preschool/kindergarten child can be encouraged to make comparative measurements. For instance, you can teach him to carefully lay his feet, toe to heel, and count how many "feet" long a room is, or how many "feet" wide the driveway is. He might measure the length of a table in "hands." Even though he is not getting a true measurement, he is learning the concept of taking measurements. Discuss the weight of objects— heavy vs. light. Ask your child to guess which is the heavier of two objects and then weigh them on a scale. A balance scale is best, as your child can observe the results without having to read numbers. Draw your child's attention to ways in which measurements are used—in building, in packaging and buying food, in weighing sand for a sandbox, in reading a map and driving, and so on.

Test. This may be the most difficult for you to deal with. A child going around tapping different objects with a spoon to hear the different sounds, may drive you a little crazy, but if you stop to realize your child's not (usually) doing it to annoy, but rather to discover something, it's easier to bear. If you encourage a child to question and measure, but don't allow him to make comparisons and test "theories," you will quickly extinguish the curiosity you worked so hard to awaken.

Almost all areas of science interest children, because they raise questions and encourage curiosity: What if I do this? Why did that move? How did that work? Children are fascinated by and love to learn the characteristics of and scientific names for things—dinosaurs, rocks, the bones of the skeleton, simple machines, clouds, and so on. Simple chemistry experiments will intrigue children, and the introduction of basic physics concepts can start children considering things in a new light.

A child can discover many basic concepts of science by simply playing with building sets of blocks and logs, and by taking apart old telephones or broken toys.

Science can also help dispel a child's fears of things like thunder or bugs, if you will make a point of studying the animal or phenomenon. The more a child understands something, the less he will fear it.

Science Activities and Experiments

K eep in mind that the results of these experiments and activities are not as important as the process through which the child must go to get the results. Encouraging curiosity means taking the time to teach your child to observe, compare, describe, and investigate. Follow up different activities with trips to the library to check out books. Encourage your child to question. Then help him find answers.

 ➡ Use pictures of animals, plants, the solar system, insects, and special sights in nature to create a stimulating environment in your young child's room.

➡ Read stories to encourage an appreciation of animals and even things like spiders (*Charlotte's Web* is great).

➡ Together, watch nature documentaries on television, and shows like PBS's *3-2-1 Contact.*

➡ Take walks and look to really *see*. Sketch, take notes. Binoculars are helpful for watching birds and large mammals. A magnifying glass helps study small animals and insects.

➡ Encourage your child to collect rocks, seeds, bones. Help him organize and label his collections.

➡ Help your child build a birdfeeder. Put it close to the house so he can observe and draw the birds. Talk about the differences in birds (size, coloring, shape) and the similarities (beaks, feathers, wings, two legs).

➡ Take time to observe and describe the weather each day. Keep a daily weather chart, drawing sun, rain, clouds to depict the weather. Help your child notice different types of clouds and introduce the names for the various types of clouds (cumulus, stratus, and so on).

➡ Let your child mix colors of paint to discover how they are related. (Blue and yellow make green, and so on.)

➡ Discuss directions: the sun rises in the east and sets in the west. Birds fly south in the winter, and north in the summer.

➡ Sound: Fill several bottles to different levels. Show your child how to blow into the tops to make different sounds, or let him tap the same bottles with a spoon to hear the different pitches produced. Have your child feel his throat and the movement of his larynx as he talks and sings.

➡ Pour a little vinegar in the bottom of a bottle with a narrow neck. Next put 2 teaspoons of baking soda into a balloon and quickly attach the balloon over the neck of the bottle. Watch as the balloon blows up! Help your child understand that a gas was formed when the soda combined with the vinegar.

➡ Help your child explore the concept of momentum. Use blocks, 2 boards, and balls. Make two ramps, one using more blocks than the other, so that it's noticeably steeper. Roll a ball down one ramp and mark the spot where the ball stopped rolling. Do the same with the other ramp and compare. What conclusions can your child draw?

➡ Compare three liquids such as water, corn syrup, and vegetable oil. Ask your child to compare smell, color, and viscosity (stickiness). Let different objects drop in each. In which liquid does a paper clip fall the slowest? the fastest?

➡ Help your child discover how air can move objects. Set a deflated balloon under an empty can. Insert a straw into the balloon and fasten with a rubber band. Using the straw, blow up the balloon and the can will move!

➡ Discuss the idea that all animals have some means of protection. For some, it's claws or speed. For others, it's camouflage, a shell, or an odor. Name different animals and see if your child can tell you its means of defense.

➡ Food dehydration: Peel and slice ripe fruit like apples or bananas, and have your child help arrange the pieces on a tray or cookie sheet which has been covered with cheesecloth. Sprinkle lemon juice over the fruit to preserve the color. (Experiment and leave a few pieces plain.) Cover with more cheesecloth and place outside in direct sunlight. Remind your child to turn the pieces of fruit twice a day and bring the tray in at night. Repeat one or two more days, until fruit is dry.

➡ To better appreciate spiders, bring a spider web home! When you locate a nice web, sprinkle it with talcum powder, and lift it carefully with a piece of black construction paper until it detaches. Spray with a spray adhesive. Take it home and discuss how the web was made and how it's used. Look for different web constructions.

➡ Magnets and compasses fascinate children. Stroke a sewing needle 30–50 times with a magnet, always in the same direction. This magnetizes the needle. Insert the needle horizontally through a cork and float it in a pan of water. Which way does the needle point? Take it out and put it back in the water. Does it point the same way? Compare the way the needle points with a compass. The needles in both should point north. Explain that this is because of the rich mineral deposits in the north which attract magnets.

➡ Have your child rub different objects together—his hands, two rocks, and so on. Introduce the term *friction* to explain the heat that results. Explain how early fires were started using this concept.

➡ Plants.
Let your child plant a small garden.
Give him a plant of his own for his room.
Have your child collect leaves and make rubbings (rub crayon over paper with a leaf underneath), or preserve leaves by pressing between two sheets of waxed paper with a warm (not hot) iron.
Press and mount dried flowers. Look them up in a flower book to find out their scientific names.
Pick and arrange flowers. Help your child appreciate beauty!

➡ Field trips. Trips to places like the airport, a nursery, a veterinarian, a factory, a weather station, a farm, and a hatchery, all serve to stimulate your child's brain to wonder, to ask questions, to contemplate answers. Field trips are a good opportunity for children to see science at work.

➡️ Growing crystals. Break up several charcoal briquets into an old pie pan. Add 2 tablespoons each of salt, water, ammonia, and bluing. As the liquid evaporates, crystals will grow.

➡️ Nests. Have your child look at real birds' nests or pictures of them. Let him collect different materials with which to try and make a nest. He might use leaves, twigs, string, mud, or clay. Encourage creativity and ingenuity.

➡️ Make a "touchy-feely bag" by placing a number of different objects in a paper sack. The greater the variety of textures and shapes, the better. See if your child can identify the objects by touch alone. Or ask him to feel for and pull out a particular object. (Objects might include: cotton ball, rock, toothpick, sponge, spoon, eraser, and so on.) As your child correctly selects an object, ask him to explain how he knew he had the right one. Try to get him to describe the textures and shapes.

➡️ Encourage your child to use his sense of touch to investigate and learn more about the world around him. Point out and offer things for him to touch. Ask him to close his eyes and describe what he feels. (Examples: the bark of various tree trunks, pussy willows, the faces and hands of the different members of your family, the skins of various fruits, and so on.)

➡️ On the next sunny day, sit outside, barefoot, for a few minutes with your child. Close your eyes, both of you, and consider the different sensations you feel. Can you feel the heat of the sun on your face? Is there a breeze? Is it cool, or warm like the sun's heat? Do you notice your hair tickling your forehead or feel prickly grass against your feet?

Ask your child to consider for a moment just how wonderful his body is with these senses that offer so much enjoyment in a world of natural richness waiting to be discovered.

CHAPTER 19

NURTURING ARTISTIC EXPRESSION

Until a child is about 6 years old, his art work reflects an "age of innocence," where drawings are pure expression, projections of his inner self. He is not yet aware of adult art conventions, and his creative being is as yet uninhibited. The *process* involved in creating art is more important and enjoyable to him than the end product of his efforts.

Although we encourage a child to draw when he is too young to express himself effectively on paper, we tend not to nurture his creativity with as much enthusiasm as he grows older. As he becomes more intellectual, the child seems to lose, to a great extent, his ability for pure expression. He becomes concerned with the end product and wants to "get it right." Consequently, he loses his spontaneity and becomes more inhibited and cautious.

This chain of events is an unfortunate one, because by not encouraging artistic expression more than we do, we deprive children of the feelings of achievement, the satisfaction they experience from having created something on their own. It is also apparent that art has terrific therapeutic potential, as it provides an outlet for children (and adults) to deal with problems which they cannot express in words.

I would urge you to do three things:

✔ Show real interest in and encourage your child's art.

✔ Provide your child with lots of art materials and make them readily available.

✔ Display his artwork. (Date and save samples regularly.)

It is helpful to know the stages a child's art goes through before he reaches the age of 6 or 7. In her article, "Kids' Art," Anne Graham describes four stages:

1 Scribbling: At this point, lines seem more important to the child than color. He does not yet understand symbolism or make "pictures."

2 Basic shapes: With improved motor control, the child can produce basic shapes, the oval being most common. He will repeat the shape and eventually add lines and circles to the interiors of the ovals.

3 Tadpoles: Once the child realizes that drawings can be symbolic, or representative, he uses his oval to make "tadpole people." These consist of a head oval and four lines projecting from it for arms and legs. As he progresses, the child may even include eyes, a nose, and a mouth inside the oval. Some may draw these facial features outside the oval, or put other body parts inside the face.

4 Combining Forms: As a child grows, his awareness of the world develops. He may begin to use another shape below the oval, to represent the body. He learns new shapes and combines them. (For example, a triangle on top of a square to represent a house.) He usually combines houses with people, making the people most important to him, bigger than the others. He notices details and adds hair, fingers, emotions. As his abilities improve further, he will probably produce dozens of pictures of the same subject, one that is especially important to him.

Around the age of 6, a child adds a setting for the images in his picture. The house sits on a lawn, people have their feet on the ground. It is at this point, when the child's understanding of the real world and his ability to draw it improve, that his art often loses its playful quality, and many children give up drawing.

No one questions the value of encouraging a child's artistic expression, but it is debatable how much a parent should try to teach his child about art. However, demonstrating techniques and drawing alongside his child, a parent can help without dictating. Below are some ideas for helping your child develop the basic skills in art, as well as a number of activity ideas using crayon, photography, paint and more.

Art Activities

 ➡ To help a child develop manual dexterity, encourage simple exercises like the following:

➡ You can show your child how to draw basic shapes—circles, triangles, squares. Add a few lines to show how a triangle suggests a sailboat, or how a circle is almost an apple. Make a point of looking at things with your child and seeing the basic shapes that one would use to draw it. Draw matchstick figures to demonstrate how one can portray action in a picture.

COLORING BOOKS.

➡ Avoid coloring books as much as possible. They eliminate the need for creativity! At the same time, so that your child isn't embarrassed when he is handed a picture to color in school, help him learn the skills of coloring. To practice "staying inside the lines," have him make a scribble in which the line crosses itself repeatedly, creating spaces. Ask your child to color inside the different spaces he made, with different colors. Show him the different results when coloring with a heavy hand and coloring lightly.

SCISSORS.

➡ You can help a child learn to use scissors by first making sure the pair you give him actually cuts easily. (If they are difficult or uncomfortable for you to use, you can't expect your child to do well either. Some children's scissors are definitely better than others.) Encourage your child to snip around the edges of small squares, then have him cut pieces (in single strokes) off long strips of paper. He will have more control later when he tries to cut out larger shapes. You can make large circles, squares or triangles for him to practice on.

PAPER BATIK.

➡ Before you begin, explain what you are going to do. Have your child soak, in water, a picture he has colored, and crumple it into a ball. Help him carefully uncrumple and flatten the paper. Blot it with paper towel and have him paint over the entire picture with a water color or diluted tempera paint. The creases in the paper absorb the paint and create an interesting effect.

ETCHING.

➡ Have your child color a piece of paper with light colored crayons. He needs to color the page completely and press hard with the crayons. Then have him cover this light coloring with a dark color, also applied heavily. (Your help in making sure the crayons are applied heavily will ensure the project's success.) Give your child a wooden toothpick or other object that is not too sharp, and let him scratch through the dark layer to uncover the light color below, creating a picture or design.

RUBBINGS.

➡ Show your child how to place a piece of paper over a flat, textured object and rub with the side of a crayon from which the paper has been removed. He can use light colors or dark, one color or more. You can suggest or provide items like keys, leaves, coins, a block of wood. Your child will probably come up with more ideas on his own.

PHOTOGRAPHIC ILLUSTRATIONS.

➡ Your child can take pictures with a camera to illustrate a story he's written. Or you might record on cassette tape, his comments as he looks at the pictures you or he took on a vacation or even a trip to the store, library, or beach. From his comments, you can help him write a story to accompany the photographs. (Other book ideas: "Here's How I Get Ready for Bed," or nursery rhymes, acted out.)

CARPENTRY.

➡ This requires *close* supervision, and quite a few tools and materials, but woodworking is a favorite of most children. Using real adult tools adds motivation, and actual construction develops in a child a sense of power over his environment. Carpentry also provides numerous opportunities to help develop skills of science, math and language arts.

• Check garage sales for tools. Your child can have his own for not too large an investment.

• Construct a sturdy workbench (24" high) and equip it with a vise or C-clamps to hold wood your child is working with. Let your child help!

• Explain to your child, the proper use and safety rules of all tools.

• Give your child roofing nails and large scraps of wood with which to practice driving nails.

• Let him drill holes and feel the heat inside caused by friction.

• Work with your child to build something he can actually use, such as bookshelves, a sandbox, a stool to help him reach the sink. Help him plan, measure, saw, hammer, and sand.

• Let your child create wood sculptures, boats, cars, houses, doll furniture, etc.

MOSAICS.

▶ Mosaics are pictures or designs created by gluing different materials onto paper, posterboard, or wood. When your child has finished a design, have him brush on a coat of white glue. There is an endless variety of possible materials which can be used to keep the activity new and interesting: canceled stamps; cereals; pieces of construction paper (squares cut with scissors or circles made with a hole punch), wallpaper, tissue paper, or crepe paper; cotton balls; seeds; macaroni; feathers; gummed stars, labels, or reinforcements; popcorn; fabric swatches; candy wrappers; dried flowers; washers; labels from cans; leaves; buttons; and so on.

NECKLACES.

▶ Use yarn (the ends stiffened with glue, nail polish, tape or melted wax) to string pieces of plastic straws, dry cereals with holes, or macaroni. Macaroni can be colored by placing it in a jar of alcohol and food coloring for a few minutes and then drying it on a paper towel.

COLLAGES.

▶ A collage is a large picture made by gluing down small pieces of many pictures which are related in some way. Help your child decide on a subject (the family, a vacation, sports, a particular sport, cars, dolls, horses, food, careers, etc.) and find pictures to include. He can look in magazines, the newspaper, or among photos you've taken. Explain that the collage will be more interesting if at least some of the pictures are in color. Homemade collages make nice gifts children can make for grandparents, teachers, and friends.

MOBILE.

▶ A mobile is a freely hanging design whose parts move in a breeze. One method of making a mobile involves cutting a clothes hanger or other wire into two pieces of equal length and crossing them to form right angles. A piece of more flexible wire twisted around the junction of the two pieces will keep them perpendicular. Suspend different objects at varying lengths from the four ends, and attach a string from the middle with which to hang the mobile from the ceiling or a light fixture.

CLAY.

➡ Give your child a lump of clay to play with. Simply squeezing, rolling and pounding it is good for developing hand muscles! Show him how to make "snakes" and how to coil them to make a bowl.

FINGERPAINTING.

➡ Put several blobs of fingerpaint on a piece of shiny paper (freezer paper works well) that has been dipped in water. Encourage your child to experiment using fingertips and palms. Some children need to be convinced that it's OK to get "dirty" and reminded that it'll all wash off!

To make your own fingerpaint, mix dry tempera paint with 1/2 cup liquid starch or liquid dishwashing detergent. Other possibilities (edible!) for fingerpaint include pudding, yogurt, and mayonnaise (add food coloring).

SLIDE PHOTOGRAPHY.

➡ Help your child (5 or 6 years old) practice taking photographs, by looking through an empty cardboard tube. Let him take pictures with an instamatic camera—use slide film—to accompany a story he's written. (He might have friends and family in costume!) He could narrate the story on cassette tape or put music to the pictures. Help your child make his slide presentation a real event, complete with popcorn, for an evening's entertainment!

DIORAMA.

➡ A diorama is a scene built into a box. Cut away one side and the top of a small sturdy cardboard box. Your child can hunt outside for materials to use to create a miniature scene—real moss, gravel, sand or dried grass to cover the ground; twigs for trees, rocks for boulders, etc. He might also use Easter grass, clay, miniature toy animals, people and cars, toothpicks, etc. Show him how he can make a tree stand up using a small lump of clay or make a tent using toothpicks and a piece of fabric or construction paper. He can paint the walls of the box blue for the sky, and for clouds, use white paint or glue whisps of cotton. Once he gets started, your child will come up with lots more ideas!

CHAPTER

13

SINGERS DANCERS AND MUSIC MAKERS

Music has always been important to me. I remember as a child, singing rounds with my family as we traveled in the car, and harmonizing with my father for fun. I was exposed to a lot of "Big Band" music, and attended a series of concerts for young people, conducted by Leonard Bernstein.

I never learned to play the piano as well as I would have liked to, but I can remember sitting on the piano bench beside my teacher as he played for me the classical pieces I was trying to master. The music was so beautiful and stirring, that I'd wish he'd play on and on and not stop.

In high school, I was a member of a large and well-disciplined chorus. It was conducted by a talented and dedicated man who was able to elicit magnificent sounds from us. I can remember feeling chills run down my spine and tears sting my eyes as I was enveloped by the music. Being a member of that chorus remains one of my warmest and most fulfilling experiences.

My college years meant loud rock, Handel and Rachmaninoff, and folk music. Each sound had a place in my life; each fulfilled a different need. That is the beauty of music!

It is up to parents to see that music has a place in his child's life. The wonderful thing about a preschooler is that, for the most part, his response to music is spontaneous and comes from deep inside, as he has not yet developed inhibitions. A melody can calm him; it can stir him to rock and sway; or it can move him to twirl and jump. He feels the rhythm, and his body responds.

It is the role of the parent to nurture this spontaneity and encourage his child's musical expression. A parent can help his child learn to appreciate different kinds of music, as well as help him make his own. Effort in both directions will contribute noticeably in the development of a well-rounded and emotionally healthy human being.

Below is a list of activities to help you nurture your child's musical creativity. Don't pressure him to sing or participate, but give plenty of opportunities and share your own joy and varied musical tastes.

Music Activities

➡ Help your child move in rhythm. Ask him to listen to music and make his body move to fit it. To encourage the development of different rhythms and responses to music, ask your child to walk: slowly, quickly, heavily, lightly, low, high, in the middle, with toes in, with toes out, on his heels, on his toes, backward, sideways, lazily, with knees high, in slow motion, happily, sadly, in the rain, in the dark, barefoot on hot pavement—all to music.

➡ We all have our own "body instruments." Help your child become aware of his and make music by clapping, whistling, humming, clicking his tongue, stamping his feet, snapping his fingers, and slapping his thighs.

➡ Make up songs or chants as you and your child do chores together, or while he is getting dressed. Encourage him to create his own. ("Gee, I like the song you made up!")

➡ Teach your child old favorites like, "This Land Is Your Land," "Yankee Doodle," "You Are My Sunshine," and so on.

➡ When your child is capable of singing a song, carrying a tune on his own, teach him how to sing in a round. Start with simple songs like "Row, Row, Row Your Boat," "Three Blind Mice," and "Frère Jacques."

➡ Sing songs with your child's name in them. Using the tune of "Mary Had a Little Lamb," for instance, you could sing, "Jenny has new rollerskates."

➡ Look for videos and records or cassettes to introduce children's songs. (See appendix)

➡️ Take your child to outdoor concerts. A child can "dance" in open space and when he's listened as long as he can, it's easy to leave.

➡️ Play different pieces of instrumental music and ask your child what animals he is reminded of. Accept any answer and ask your child to explain his choice.

INSTRUMENTS YOU CAN MAKE

➡️ Strum a piece of corrugated cardboard with a spoon.

➡️ Use two kettle lids with knobs as cymbals.

➡️ Hummers: On one end of a cardboard tube, make a hole with a paper punch. Make the hole as far from the end of the tube as the handle of the paper punch will allow. Cover that end with a 3" square of waxed paper or aluminum foil. Secure the square with an elastic band. Be sure not to cover the hole you punched. Encourage your child to decorate his instrument, and show him how to put his mouth up to the open end and blow and hum into it at the same time.

➡️ Triangle: Tie a string around the head of a large (5") nail. While holding on to the string, tap the nail with a "striker," a 4" nail.

➡️ Drums can be as simple as an empty oatmeal box and a wooden spoon. You can also cover a bowl or coffee can with inner tube material or real drum skin. (Secure tightly!) Make a drum stick by covering the end of a stick or piece of dowel with fabric-covered foam.

➡️ Maracas: Put a little rice in a lightweight plastic bottle, and some dried beans in another. Shake alternately.

➡️ Tambourine: Put a handful of dried beans in a small foil pie pan. Lay another pie pan over it, tape around the edges, and shake!

WHAT ABOUT TELEVISION?

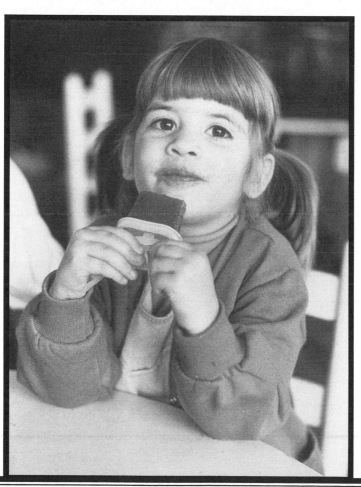

I once saw a cartoon in a well-known magazine which showed, in a series of drawings, the effect on a family of a week without television—the result of a school experiment. Far from inspiring laughter, the cartoon was depressing and discouraging, to me anyway. The family in the cartoon was simply lost without the "boob tube" to entertain. I can't help feeling this to be a sorry statement about the degree to which many of us let the television take over our lives.

I bring up this issue because I am concerned about the level of questioning, creativity, and self-sufficiency in our children. I, too, watch television, and will admit that I honestly enjoy a few favorite shows. But, too often, I find myself watching something inane simply because it's there. When I ask myself, "Will I really be missing something valuable if I don't see this show?", the answer is invariably no. I do believe there are worthwhile programs to be seen and encourage you to make a point of watching shows like *National Geographic* specials, *Sesame Street*, and the news with your child. Watch for programs of interest on your Public Broadcasting System (PBS) station.

I would also encourage you to decide which of the shows that are purely for entertainment your family could pass up. Granted, there are definitely times when pure entertainment is necessary—we all need to relax and to laugh—but I think we would all be surprised by how little television we really need.

Those of my students who watch television a lot seem to be generally more passive and less energetic or motivated than those students who spend their free time reading, pursuing hobbies, participating in sports, 4-H, scouting, or simply playing outdoors. I would like to ask you to consider the following three questions:

❶ Are you really aware of how many hours your child spends watching television?

❷ Do you make sure you know what he watches?

❸ Are you happy about your child watching as much television as he does?

You might be surprised and dismayed by the answer to #1 if you were to actually keep track for a week or so. If you answered #2 with a no, you might also be surprised and upset by the true answer. Whether you answered #3 with a yes or no, I would like to present some information, and suggestions, in an effort to encourage you to consider your own situation as far as television is concerned, and possibly alter it somewhat.

While there are a few exceptions, an overwhelming majority of the research on children and television finds that time spent by children (particularly preschoolers) watching television is not only wasted, but undoubtedly harmful. The list of bad effects is a long one, but perhaps the single most valid point to be made is the one made by Paul Copperman, author of *The Literary Hoax*, when he asks parents to consider what a child misses during those hours he spends in front of the T.V. screen. "He is not working in the garage with his father, or in the garden with his mother. He is not doing homework, or reading, or collecting stamps. He is not cleaning his room, washing the supper dishes, or cutting the lawn. He is not listening to a discussion about community politics among his parents and their friends. He is not playing baseball or going fishing, or painting pictures. *Exactly what does television offer that is so valuable that it can replace all these activities?*"

In *The Read-Aloud Handbook*, Jim Trelease describes other things television does for our children: Television interrupts the most important language lesson in the child's life—family conversation. It stifles the imagination, and desensitizes the child's sense of sympathy for suffering. Television presents material in a manner opposite to that of a classroom—visually as opposed to verbally—and fosters a short attention span.

John Rosemond, author of *Parent Power!*, feels there are many ways in which T.V. harms a child's chances for success in school. A child who is used to seeing scenes shift on the average of every 4 seconds, as they do on television, is sure to be bored in a classroom, and as a result, his eyes bounce around the room, in an attempt to reestablish the level of stimulation he's grown used to. His attention span, then, is extremely short, his ability to listen and look carefully, almost nonexistent.

Rosemond, as do others, points out that watching television trains ones eyes to stare, rather than to scan. Scanning is an important skill needed in learning to read. With pupils fixed, hands limp in his lap, a child is simply a spectator in front of the television. Watching television requires no learning; you just do it—or more to the point, you just don't do anything else. Play, on the other hand, involves exploration, activity, and fantasy. Reading, too, requires involvement; it is an active, problem-solving exercise.

A third and interesting viewpoint, on the subject of children and television, comes from Fred Rogers (of the T.V. show "Mister Rogers"), who with Barry Head wrote *Mr. Rogers Talks With Parents.* While Rogers feels the potential for good programming exists, and while he tries hard on his own show to communicate with children those things he feels are important, he states his opinion that "until change comes from within the industry, television will continue to have a negative effect on children, family life, and human relationships in general."

Rogers worries that while television stimulates a child's inner feelings (raises doubts, fears, questions, emotions) it does not help him *deal* with these things. He feels that only if parents will watch shows with a child can these inner feelings and questions be dealt with effectively.

Violence, in particular, whether on shows or the news, can hurt a child's emotional growth. Rogers encourages parents to use commercials and the time between programs to help their children cope with what they see by asking questions ("why do you think that happened? what do you think will happen next?") and sometimes making clear value statements ("that's not the way it should be; that's not the right thing to do"). It can also be reassuring to encourage your child to look for all the helpers in a tragic or disaster situation.

If you and your child are going to watch a lot of television, it would probably help if you followed Roger's suggestions and discussed the shows as thoroughly as possible. If you are beginning to wonder if there isn't a better solution, you might consider the one used by Jim Trelease, or your own version of it.

Trelease advocates strong parental control of the T.V., which he admits is more easily said than done. When his children were ages 5 and 9, he and his wife created a new house law: no T.V. on school nights. It was *extremely* difficult to stick to, as there were tears, pressures, and pleading for literally months.

But if you can resist the tears and calmly answer the questions, chances are that you will see changes similar to those Trelease saw occur in his own house. After three months, suddenly there was time in the evenings to read aloud as a family, do homework without hurrying, learn to play chess, play a sport, draw, paint, and TALK.

Eventually the plan was modified in the Trelease home to: no T.V. after supper until bedtime, Monday through Thursday; and each child is allowed to watch one schoolnight show a week (subject to parent approval). This last proved valuable as it forces the children to be discriminating.

The one major hurdle in such a plan is that if you decide to curtail your child's television viewing and create a 3-hour void, you must make a commitment to fill that void. You must produce paper and crayons, teach how to play checkers, help with baking cookies, go to the library for new books, and make yourself available for talk.

In many households, television never becomes an issue because it is not considered a priority or reward. It is simply there, and mostly unused. In other families, television time can be decreased, not by setting rules, but rather by providing appealing alternatives which encourage the child to voluntarily shake the T.V. habit.

Alternatives to Television

➡ Invest in a pad of drawing paper and start your child sketching. Have him try pencil, charcoal, pastels, and attempt different subjects.

➡ Borrow, buy, or rent a musical instrument. Your child might be a musician!

➡ Get out a deck of cards and teach your child "Old Maid," "Go Fish," "War," or "Concentration."

➡ Charades are a lot of fun if you can let go and be a little silly. Even a 4- or 5-year-old can participate.

➡ Search in your closet for or invest in board games like "Candyland," "Rack-O," "Memory," or checkers. Older children usually enjoy games like "Sorry," "Clue," "Parcheesi."

➡ Set up a family reading hour or half-hour, when everyone curls up in a comfortable place and reads (or has read to him), a book, magazine, comic book, encyclopedia—anything, as long as it's reading. Make popcorn afterward and talk about what you've read.

➡ Go bowling or play miniature golf once in a while if you can. Try croquet, tetherball, ping pong, or hopscotch.

➡ Take a walk or bike ride as a family.

➡ Bake cookies. Experiment with new recipes!

➡ Work in the garden or rake the lawn—together.

➡ Write silly stories and read them to each other. With children too young to write, make up silly stories aloud.

CHAPTER

15

Summer:
DEALING WITH
"MOM, WHAT CAN I DO?"

Not even two weeks into summer vacation, I ran into one of my next year's students in the grocery store. "How's your summer going?" I asked.

"OK," she answered without much conviction. "Kind of boring sometimes," she admitted after a slight hesitation.

No doubt a few of you have heard similar words and slightly plaintive voices asking, "Ma, what can I do now?"

I ran across an interesting solution to the problem in *Redbook* magazine. Cherie Taylor Pedersen had a plan ready for her four children when summer began. She turned four pieces of 9" × 12" posterboard into personal charts for her children, and divided each into different areas of achievement, or goals, depending on the individual and his age. Mrs. Pedersen bought humorous stickers to place on the charts for each goal achieved.

Yes, but would a child really want to do something like this? I think so, for a number of reasons. First, because it's an answer to "Ma, what can I do now?" Second, it's something new and different. Third, for some reason, small children love stickers—perhaps because they are such tangible proof of accomplishment, and accomplishment means a reason to feel good about oneself. Who doesn't like that? Last of all, you can provide the final reason, a special reward promised if your child completes his chart.

Discuss at the beginning of the project, what your child would like to do when the goals have been achieved. Mrs. Pedersen's children knew they wanted to visit a farm where miniature horses were raised, and that's what they did. You could suggest a visit to a special place, a night at the movies, or a day canoeing, but your child will probably come up with his own goal if you give him time. As long as it's within reason, try to go along with his idea.

To me, this approach to summer is an excellent one, because it provides structure, sets goals within attainable limits, and offers incentive in the bonus of a tangible reward. If you want to try it, all you need are the charts, the stickers and a plan. The goals can be whatever seems appropriate and reasonable for your child. To complete the chart, each area might require three or four stickers. You would need to post a target date or deadline, by which all the chart's goals must be completed in order to earn the special reward.

When thinking about what you'd like to see your child accomplish, you might want to consider the following possible goals. They offer some ideas to choose from, but you will probably come up with some on your own which would be as good or better for your child. Keep in mind his individual capabilities. If he has attended kindergarten, and his teacher has reported that he is weak in certain skills, this is a good way to work on them.

Choose goals which create a sense of challenge and will ensure a feeling of accomplishment. Be careful not to set goals which are unreasonable and which risk causing despair and frustration.

For the non-reader, use pictures and/or words to label goals:

✔ Pick up clothes every day.

✔ Help Mom cook dinner.

✔ Learn to hit a ball (throw, or catch a ball, jump rope, skip, etc.).

✔ Learn a new song and sing it to the family.

✔ Put away toys before bed.

✔ Build, make, or collect something.

✔ Do an extra job around the house.

For the child who can read and write, in addition to the goals above:

✔ Read a book within a certain time frame.

✔ Copy the alphabet, write 5 words, a letter, or a story.

✔ Memorize a poem (or 2 jokes or 2 riddles) and recite it at dinner.

✔ Learn to count and/or write to 20 (50, 100; or learn addition or subtraction facts—2's one week, 3's the next—be realistic as far as what your child can handle and still enjoy).

One additional goal to consider would be to "Have each week a warm fuzzy for each member of the family." If this goal was on each child's chart, it would be a nice excuse to create a special weekly family meeting for sharing warm fuzzies. (Warm fuzzies are things said or done to make a person feel good about himself. A hug is a warm fuzzy. Telling the cook that his or her meal was delicious is a warm fuzzy. Or you can "give someone a warm fuzzy" for helping with the weeding, or for learning to swim underwater. If at weekly family meetings, people "gave" each other warm fuzzies, having had a week to watch for reasons, it seems inevitable that spontaneous warm fuzzies would soon increase in number.)

What's so nice about this whole idea is that all you have to provide is the motivation to get your child started, the chart and the stickers, lots of encouragement, and a reward at the end. You can feel good knowing that you'll be encouraging your child to improve on important and worthwhile skills, while doing some creative thinking. You'll also be providing your child with an opportunity to see himself accomplish some goals, and thus, feel good about himself.

If your child's attitude becomes negative or his efforts only half-hearted, you need to sit down with him and discuss why the activity isn't working. Either the goals are not appropriate or the reward doesn't provide enough incentive. Remember that your attitude toward the whole idea is extremely important. Your own enthusiasm is the key.

COURTNEY GOALS:	June 15-21	June 22-28	June 29-July 5	July 6-12
1. Pick up my clothes every day				
2. Practice P.E. skill every day (15 minutes)				
3. Help Mom cook 2 dinners				
4. Make, build or collect something				
5. Learn a riddle each day or 2 poems/week				
6. Have a warm fuzzy for each family member				
7. Learn to count to	20	30	40	50

Making Summer a Special Time for the Family

While it's nice to keep a child busy during the long days of summer, it is also important that he be allowed to enjoy that special sense of freedom that comes with a vacation. This is especially important for the school-age child who, at least occasionally, needs to have several hours at a time where he can feel carefree and is completely in charge of determining how his time is to be spent.

Making summer special can be especially difficult when both parents work and the child is in some type of day care, as is so common today. Take advantage of the long daylight hours and warm weather to do things as a family which you can't do during the colder months of the year. Barbecue as much as possible and eat supper outdoors. Try eating breakfast outdoors for a fun change. After dinner, take walks or bike rides as a family. Invest in a tetherball, badminton, or croquet game and *join* your children in friendly competition. You could invite the neighbors and match teams of parent/child against each other.

Weekends are usually the best time for more "special" activities. Plan ahead and schedule trips to famous landmarks, historical sites, museums, an amusement park, the zoo, the city (if you live in the country) or the country (if you live in the city), a beach, lake, or river. It's not uncommon for people to never visit "tourist attractions" in their own area, (I lived in southern California for six years before I ever visited Disneyland) but if they attract tourists, maybe they're worth a visit!

Consider doing some hiking and camping. Children love to gather wood for a fire, pitch a tent, roast marshmallows, and sleep in sleeping bags. A clear night provides an opportunity to do some star-gazing. Camping also sets the stage for imagining life long ago. Ask your child to consider what it was like living in the time when families traveled west in covered wagons and settled in areas far from others. What does he think he would like about living during those days? What would he dislike?

A summer would be an especially memorable one if you, *as a family*, got involved in something *new*. It could be a sport or activity which you may have wanted to try but had never gotten around to. Present a few ideas to the rest of the family and take a vote. Make a plan to pursue this new activity at least twice a month. You might consider sailing, horseback riding, camping, hiking, canoeing, tennis, snorkeling, fishing, rollerskating, bowling. You might take up jogging or try photography and set up a darkroom.

People who learn something together inevitably develop a sense of camaraderie. It is also extremely valuable for your child to see his parents making mistakes, laughing at them, learning from them, and having fun. Finding yourself in a situation where you are learning something new will also remind you of the challenge your child faces repeatedly as he attempts to learn new skills.

Swimming and Water Safety

Swimming involves the use of most of the body's muscles and is excellent cardiovascular exercise. As a result, it is wonderful exercise for children (and adults). Children tend to burn up a tremendous amount of energy just playing in the water, and sleep particularly well after an afternoon of swimming.

In addition to its contributions to a child's physical well-being, swimming offers him a chance to feel good about himself. Each new skill he learns can be an excuse to celebrate! Knowing he can succeed in one area of his life, a child will feel positive about his ability to meet other challenges.

Summer is the ideal time to enroll your child in swimming lessons and water safety classes. Besides being something most children love to do, swimming is also a valuable skill to master for reasons of safety. In addition, an afternoon of swimming can be a wonderful time for a parent to play with his child.

While lessons are not a must, they can be helpful to a parent who is not an experienced swimmer himself or who would like to know how to help his child learn to swim. Lessons are even more valuable for a child over 5 who has had little experience in the water and has had longer to develop a mistrust of the water. They are also helpful for a child who can dog paddle and is ready to learn other strokes.

Don't postpone swimming instruction indefinitely. If you don't live near a swimming area, look into the "Y" or community pool. Sooner or later, your child will be with children who are strong swimmers, and he'll be much safer if he has a solid swimming background. The American Red Cross runs many summer swimming programs nationwide.

The first job facing the parent of an infant or toddler is introducing the child to and helping him feel at home in the water. In the beginning, this means the parent keeping the child close to his body, in a firm hold, so that the child feels completely safe. Over a period of visits to the swimming area, the parent can release his hold a bit, as his child's hands begin to cling less tightly and his body begins to relax in the water. Boats or water toys help make the pool a place to play.

Once a child is happy to be in the water and will splash and kick and attempt to blow bubbles, he will probably welcome a little independence. At this point, I would suggest investing in a device which holds the child upright and allows him to float and kick and paddle. The device will not only give the child a sense of freedom, it will relieve the parent's back as well!

Usually by the age of 3, the child is ready to graduate to "floaties" which inflate around his upper arms. He will delight in watching his parent go underwater and pop back up, do handstands, or a cannonball! If he is shown how to hold his breath and close his mouth, he will soon learn to go underwater without fear. (Most prefer swimming underwater once they learn how.) Placing a toy, golf ball, or rock on the bottom step of a pool can provide a reason for the child to go underwater. After he's become comfortable with this activity, he will enjoy retrieving objects in deeper water.

A parent who is willing to get in the water, play with and encourage his child, can help his child progress to swimming completely on his own.

Long Car Trips: A Few Tips

➡ Explain ahead of time where you'll be going. Show your child on a map its location, and the route you'll take to get there.

➡ Help prepare a young child for the length of time to be spent in the car. "A trip to the store is a short trip. This will be much longer. We will be in the car for as long as you used to spend in school each day."

➡ Take along something familiar (a favorite toy or book) as well as crayons, pencils and paper, and games for individuals and a group. If there's room, a small pillow and small blanket are comforting as well as comfortable.

➡ Sing songs as a family.

➡ Plan adequate stops for rest and exercise.

➡ Give your child things to look for. Make a game of finding things as you drive. Have them count the number of red cars, the number of exit signs, etc.

➡ Take along easy to eat snacks and cold juices.

➡ Play " 'A' My Name is Alice." (*A* my name is *Alice* and my brother's name is *Al*. We come from *Alaska*, and we sell *apples*.) The next person uses "B," and so on.

➡ Play "Who Am I?" The child decides who he is (president, actress, book character, aunt, friend— anyone living or dead), and others in the car ask questions which can be answered "Yes" or "No" only, to establish who he is. The correct guesser gets to be the next to give clues.

Other Summer Activities

➡ Use the summer to take your own "field trips." Go to different places to see how things work, and how products are made. Try a veterinarian's office, an ice cream factory, a farm, a newspaper, a printer, a computer distributor, ferryboat, the airport, a nursery or greenhouse.

➡ Try to make regular visits to the library. Let your child get his own library card if he doesn't already have one. Encourage him to choose different kinds of books.

➡ This would be a good time to help your child choose a magazine he particularly likes and subscribe to it. It would provide regular mail and encourage reading.

➡ If you have space in your yard, it might be fun for your child to have a small garden of his own. Even if time slips by and it's too late for certain vegetables, there are those which would still grow. Try radishes, greentail onions, lettuce, pumpkins, zucchini. Your child will be so proud of himself and will "check" his plants many times a day. This is a particularly nice activity to work on together.

➡ For little children, sometimes it's nice just to be able to keep their hands occupied. Play dough is an easy way to do just that. Once it's made, it will keep well if stored in an airtight container, and it will provide hours of fun if handed out along with various kitchen utensils. Below is one version of how to make your own play dough:

1/2 cup salt	**1 cup water**
1 cup flour	**1 Tbs. vegetable oil**
2 Tbs. cream of tartar	**food coloring**

Mix salt, flour, and cream of tartar together. Add water, oil, and food coloring. Cook mixture on medium heat until dough feels right (3–5 minutes). Store in a plastic bag or container with lid.

➡ Use every opportunity available to include your child in your activities. When repairing a leaky faucet, fixing the car, laying a new floor tile, working in the garden or baking cookies, make him feel lucky and important to be helping you. Take time to explain what you're doing and the names of the tools. Also explain any safety rules when appropriate.

➡ You can encourage even a preschooler's curiosity by giving him discarded hinges, locks, old doorbells and so on, to investigate and manipulate. (Check first for any small parts which might get put in a mouth.)

➡ If you notice an interest, encourage your child to start a collection. Help him find a "display case" of some kind—an old drawer, a box, an inexpensive picture frame.

➡ Go outside and practice basic motor skills like throwing and catching a ball. (See chapter 9 for more ideas.)

➡ Visit ethnic restaurants if available, or cook ethnic foods. Have children compare foods, eating styles, table settings, traditions. Try Italian, Japanese, French, Greek, Vietnamese, Ethiopian, Mexican, Chinese, etc. If you can, call ahead and go early (before lunch), and watch some of the preparation.

➡ Try different modes of transportation: canoes, sailboats, ferryboats, trains, and for a huge treat, if possible, a hot air balloon or helicopter. Visit airports, docks, train depots. Read books appropriate to each week's visit.

ENTERING KINDERGARTEN

For most children, entering kindergarten is both an exciting and frightening experience. It means going to school "like the big kids," but it also means separation from all that is familiar and safe. A child's entrance into kindergarten also raises a number of questions for parents to consider.

What Is The Right Age?

One of the most controversial questions has been "What is the optimal age for a child to enter kindergarten?" Studies have shown that more important than a child's actual age, is his age *relative to the rest of the class.* A child who is considerably younger than his peers is at a disadvantage as far as social and emotional adjustment are concerned. Poor social adjustment tends to result in negative behavior and responses, as well as a lowering of self-esteem. Consequently, the child's chances for success in school decrease.

Research has shown that where there is no screening done, the academic achievement of a child who is younger than his peers suffers. In cases where stringent screening procedures allowed only children with exceptional ability to enter school at a younger age than the rest of the class, the students tended to perform as well as, or better than their normal age classmates. However, *these younger children still appear to achieve at a lower level than would be anticipated for them at that grade level if they had waited a year.*

Schools have recently been raising the age requirement for entering kindergarten. Certainly there are a number of other factors to consider—mental age, social maturity, and prior school experience—but I have no doubt that, if there is any question, *it is far better to wait an extra year than put your child in a situation for which he may not be ready.*

The Kindergarten Experience

The concept of kindergarten has changed considerably during recent years. With more households having both parents working, a greater number of children are exposed to group situations and learning activities at an earlier age. These socialization skills and group activities used to be provided for the first time, by kindergarten. Now, when a child enters kindergarten, he is often ready for more academic activities. Thus, the tendency is to increase the number of academic activities included in the kindergarten curriculum. This should be acceptable as long as each child is considered as an individual. This is always the greatest, but most important challenge any teacher faces—to fit the educational program to the child and not vice versa.

It is important for the parent to make a point of talking with the child's teacher. What is her philosophy concerning the role of kindergarten? What does she do with a child who is academically ahead of the other children? or a child who is behind?

While you want your child's intellect to be challenged during kindergarten, keep in mind the value of the more traditional kindergarten activities. An effective teacher will combine the two in the way that best suits the needs of her particular class. Certainly a parent who acknowledges the value of providing experiences for his child in and around the home before he enters school, will accept the importance of providing an abundance of "non-academic" discovery experiences in school. These include playing house, building with blocks, singing, dancing, climbing on a jungle gym.

If, for some reason, you feel your child's kindergarten experience is not providing what it should be, there are several things you should do. First, take a day to visit your child's class and simply observe. You might also observe a kindergarten in another school or another class in the same school. *Keep an open mind* and watch how the teacher interacts with the children, how your child relates to her and to his classmates. Chances are, a day in the classroom will put your mind at ease.

If you have questions, ask the teacher when you could meet with her to discuss them. You have a right and a need to express concerns—this is your child you're talking about!—but also, try to listen objectively to the teacher's responses. Remember that she has spent years studying to become a teacher, and there are reasons behind her methods.

If, after meeting with the teacher, you still are not satisfied with the education your child is receiving, meet with the school principal and explain your feelings. While one parent's complaint will not and should not justify changing a teacher's style or moving a child to another class, it deserves recognition and investigation by the principal. Complaints by numerous parents should prompt more serious attention. It is possible that your child's teacher is incompetent. (No doubt there are those in my profession who will not appreciate my making such a statement.) It's also possible that your child and his teacher are a mismatch. And, too, it may be that your expectations are inappropriate given the age and stage of development of your child. All of these possibilities need to be examined. First and foremost, approach the school staff—teacher, principal, classroom aides—as a support team interested in what's best for your child. If you avoid the adversarial position (unless it is clearly warranted), your child is likely to benefit from the joint effort on his behalf.

Hopefully, the relationship you and your child develop with his teacher will be a positive one. The majority of teachers went into education because they honestly enjoy working with children. It is important that you let your child's teacher know a little about you and your family life, so that she can better understand your child's behavior and respond to it in the most appropriate way. For kindergarteners, it is helpful to let the teacher know about any family situations that might impact on your child's behavior.

Make a real effort to attend all parent/teacher conferences and open house. Consider attending meetings of the local school board and Parent-Teacher Association (PTA). If the PTA is not currently very active, perhaps it's time to change that! A PTA can be a wonderfully effective means of supporting and improving the education in a school district.

If you have any free time, ask your child's teacher if she would like parent volunteers to help out in the classroom. If she says "yes," you might offer to contact the other parents and help set up a volunteer schedule. If a teacher can count on an extra adult at certain times, she can plan activities that she might not otherwise be able to manage or manage as effectively.

Ask, too, what you can be doing at home to help your child. If you do your part to keep the lines of communication open, it will be to your child's benefit.

Preparing Your Child For Kindergarten

Kindergarteners are wonderfully excitable and enthusiastic. A major part of a child's reaction to school comes from his teacher, obviously, but a child's expectations and anticipatory feelings come from his parents' attitudes.

There are many things a parent can do to make the experience a success.

➡ Most schools have a kindergarten visiting day before school starts, to familiarize the children with the school, their classroom, and teacher. If your school doesn't have such an introduction day, arrange to walk through the halls with your child and see his classroom. A good time would be just before school ends for the summer prior to his entrance into kindergarten. Once a child knows where he is going, a lot of the apprehension he feels will disappear.

➡ Your child should be able to take care of his personal needs—dress himself, tie his shoes, button and zip clothing, buckle his belt, and use a kleenex. Work on these over the summer, but be aware that tying and zippers are skills that come later to some children.

➡ See that your child has sufficient sleep and a good breakfast each day. Send him to school every morning with a hug, a kiss, a few words of praise ("You look great today!", "You brushed your hair nicely this morning!"), and a cheery parting.

➡ Your child should know his full name—not just his first or nickname. Be sure he knows the difference.

➡ Your child should know his address (house number and street) and phone number. If he doesn't, write it on a slip of paper and tuck it in his pocket.

➡ Prepare your child for the length of time he will be away from home and from you. Help him become aware of the clock and idea of a morning, noon, and afternoon.

➡ Familiarize your child with the route home from school. Tell him who will be waiting for him after school, be it at the school bus stop or home or the babysitter's.

➡ Break in new shoes ahead of time. It's hard to learn new things in a new environment if you've got blisters on your feet!

➡ If your child will be riding a bus, try to find someone he knows—perhaps an older neighbor—who will sit with him the first few days.

➡ Your child should have a physical before starting school to be sure he is fine—general health, ears, eyes, up-to-date immunizations.

➡ Your child could use a small knapsack or carry-all for bringing home papers and jackets, etc. Stick in a surprise sticker when he needs a boost, and dry socks and mittens when the weather is inclement.

➡ Skills to work on with a preschooler:
counting to 10
counting objects
naming colors
reciting the alphabet
cutting with scissors
drawing a man
copying a square
printing his name
understanding opposites: hot/cold, up/down,
heavy/light, and so on.

If your child hasn't mastered some of these skills, don't embarrass him, but continue working on them with him. If you feel you are making little or no progress, arrange a conference with his preschool or kindergarten teacher.

Be sure your child doesn't think he is going to learn to read during the first day or week of school. I have heard a number of stories about children who have been sadly disappointed by school when they expected to and didn't become readers "overnight." Before starting school, they may hear from well-meaning relatives and adults, words like, "Aren't you getting big! You're going to school, and you're going to learn to read!" Gently make him aware of the fact that the process of learning to read takes time, but it is fun, and you will help him all you can.

This first year of formal education is critical to the development of your child's attitude toward learning and school. Be sure to give it the attention it deserves, and don't let difficult situations go on for too long. Your involvement in and contributions to your child's education may perhaps not seem as intense once he enters school, but you definitely need to continue to participate in his learning and his development as an emotionally healthy human being. Every event, every project in school opens possibility for family discussion, "help" on difficult activities, and supportiveness. In many ways, your involvement will be greater than ever as your child's interests evolve. A parent's job is not an easy one, but there surely are few which are more fulfilling.

BIBLIOGRAPHY

Anderson, Susan and James L. Hoot. "Kids, Carpentry and the Preschool Classroom," **Day Care and Early Education**, Vol. 13, No. 3, Spring 1986.

Beck, Joan. **Best Beginnings: Giving Your Child A Head Start in Life**, New York: G.P. Putnam's Sons, 1983.

Brayman, R. and W. Piersel. "The Early Entrance Option: Academic and Social/Emotional Outcomes;" **Psychology in the Schools**, Vol. 24, April 1987.

Briggs, Dorothy Corkille. **Your Child's Self-Esteem**, Garden City, N.Y.: Doubleday & Co., Inc., 1970.

Broughton, Connie. "When Mother's Intuition Isn't Enough", **Redbook Magazine**, May 1982.

Brown, Sam. **Bubbles, Rainbows & Worms: Science Experiments for Pre-School Children**, Mt. Rainier, Maryland: Gryphon House, Inc., 1981.

Canfield, Jack and Harold Wells. **100 Ways to Enhance Self-Concept in the Classroom**, Englewood Cliffs, New Jersey: Prentice-Hall, 1976.

Church, Ellen Booth. "Fun Graphs," **Day Care and Early Education**, Vol. 14, No. 2, Winter 1986.

Copperman, Paul. **The Literary Hoax**, New York: William Morrow and Co., 1978.

Dodson, Dr. Fitzhugh. **How To Parent**, New York: Nash Publishing, 1970.

Doman, Glenn. **How To Teach Your Baby To Read**, New York: Random House,1964. **Teach Your Baby Math**, New York: Simon & Schuster, 1979.

Edwards, Betty. **Drawing On the Right Side of the Brain: A Course in Enhancing Creativity and Artistic Confidence**, Los Angeles: J.P. Tarcher, Inc., 1979.

Elkind, David. **The Hurried Child: Growing Up Too Fast Too Soon**, Reading, Mass., Addison-Wesley Publishing Co., 1981.

Forgan, Harry. **Help Your Child Learn To Read**, Toronto: Paguarian Press, 1975.

Glenn, J.A., Editor. **Children Learning Geometry: Foundation Activities in Shape—A Handbook for Teachers**, London: Harper & Row, Publishers, 1979.

Gordon, Ira, Barry Guinagh, and R. Emile Jester. **Child Learning Through Child Play: Learning Activities for 2 & 3 Year Olds**, New York: St. Martin's Press, 1972.

Graham, Anne. "Kids' Art," **Parents Magazine**, Feb. 1985.

Haas, Carolyn Buhai. "Science and Nature Projects," **Day Care and Early Education**, Vol. 13, No. 4, Summer 1986.

Hauswald, Carol. "Rainy Days and Mondays," **Parents Magazine**, February 1986.

Institute for Creative Education (ICE). "Brainstorming and Creative Thinking," a workshop, Sewell, New Jersey, 1982.

Johnson, June. **838 Ways to Amuse a Child: Crafts, Hobbies, and Creative Ideas For Children from 6–12**, New York: Harper Colophon Books, 1983.

Jones, Sandy. **Learning For Little Kids: A Parent's Sourcebook for the Years 3 to 8**, Boston: Houghton Mifflin Co., 1979.

Koenke, Karl. "Handwriting Instruction: What Do We Know?", **The Reading Teacher**, Vol. 40, No. 2, November 1986.

Larrick Nancy. **A Parent's Guide to Children's Reading**, New York: Doubleday & Co., Inc., 1958.

Leman, Dr. Kevin. **Parenthood Without Hassles (Well Almost)**, Irvine, California: Harvest House Publishers, 1979.

Levine, Carolyn Anne. **Knockout Knock Knocks**, New York: E.P. Dutton, 1978.

Lewis, Claudia. **A Big Bite of the World: Children's Creative Writing**, Englewood Cliffs, New Jersey: Prentice-Hall, inc., 1979.

Maucione, Jeff. "Integrating Literature Into a Child's Therapy Program", A workshop.

Mayesky, Mary, Donald Neuman, and Raymond Wlodkowski. **Creative Art for Young Children**, Albany, New York: Delmar Publishers, Inc., 1975.

McKie, Roy. **The Riddle Book**, New York: Random House, 1978.

Miller, Mary Susan. **Bringing Learning Home**, New York: Harper & Row, Publishers, 1981.

Neel, Dr. Rick. "Roadblocking: A Game to Make Frustration Fun", **Teaching Exceptional Children**, 7 (I), 19, Fall 1974.

Neel, R.S. & S. Winslow. "A Developmental Sequence For Teaching Social Behaviors," **Pointer**, 20 (2), 1975.

Pedersen, Cherie Taylor. "How I Coped With the 'What can we do now, Mom?' Summer Doldrums", **Redbook**, July 1982.

Pehrsson, Dr. Robert. "Writing Skills for the Elementary Grades," a workshop.

Pehrsson, Robert S. and H. Alan Robinson. **The Semantic Organizer Approach to Writing and Reading Instruction**, Gaithersburg, Maryland: Aspen Publishers, Inc., 1985.

Reimer, Judith. "The Whole Rainy Day Catalog," **Parents Magazine**, September 1986.

Rogers, Fred with Barry Head. **Mr. Rogers Talks With Parents**, New York: Berkley Books, 1983.

Rosemond, John. **Parent Power! A Common Sense Approach to Raising Your Children in the Eighties.** New York: Pocket Books, 1981.

Schoolfield, Lucille and Josephine Timberlake. **The Phonovisual Method**, Washington, D.C.: Phonovisual Products, 1964.

Sharp, Evelyn. **Thinking Is Child's Play**, New York: Avon Books, 1969.

Smethurst, Wood. **Teaching Young Children To Read At Home**, New York: McGraw-Hill Book Co., 1975.

Sprung, Barbara, Merle Froschl, and Patricia Campbell. "What Will Happen If
. . . Young Children and the Scientific Method," **Day Care and Early
Education**, Vol. 13, No. 4, Summer 1986.

Stecher, Miriam. "Music All Day Long," **Parents Magazine**, June 1985.

Steiner, Claude. **A Warm Fuzzy Tale**, Rolling Hills Esttaes, California: Jalmar
Press, 1977.

Stinar, Raymond. "Helping Your Child to Develop Body Skills," an article in
Learning For Little Kids by Sandy Jones, Boston:
Houghton Mifflin Co. 1979.

"Teaching Tips From Teachers!" Rochester, New York:
Eastman Kodak Co., 1979.

Trelease, Jim. **The Read-Aloud Handbook**, New York:
Penguin Handbooks, 1982.

Vitale, Barbara Meister. **Unicorns Are Real: A Right-Brained Approach to
Learning**, Rolling Hills Estates, California: Jalmar Press, 1982.

Wharton, Susan (research and text). **Children's Crafts** by the Editors of Sunset
Books & Sunset Magazine, Menlo Park, California:
Lane Publishing Co., 1976.

Wiener, Harvey. **Any Child Can Write: How To Improve Your Child's Writing
Skills**, New York: McGraw-Hill Book Co., 1978.

Wolfgang, Mary E. and Corinne Mullen. **I'm Ready To Learn: Activities For
Preschool and Kindergarten Children**, Malvern, Pennsylvania:
Instructo/McGraw-Hill, 1983.

Zaidenberg, Arthur. **Your Child Is An Artist**, New York: Grosset & Dunlop
Publishers, 1949.

APPENDIX

There are quite a few books on parenting which offer lists of resources to use with your child. Rather than repeat what you can find elsewhere, I would like to offer, instead, a few not-so-well-known resources along with some well-known favorites.

BOOKS WHICH DISCUSS RIGHT VS LEFT HEMISPHERE OF THE BRAIN

Unicorns are Real: A Right-Brained Approach to Learning, by Barbara Meister Vitale (Jalmar Press, 1982). This book explains how the two hemispheres of the brain work, offers three screening methods to help determine a child's dominant hemisphere, and lots of activities which involve the use of the right hemisphere of the brain.

Drawing on the Right Side of the Brain: A Course in Enhancing Creativity and Artistic Confidence, by Betty Edwards (J.P. Tarcher, Inc., 1979). While the activities in this book are meant for teaching art to upper elementary children and anyone older, the introductory chapters offer a good explanation of hemisphericity. This book is wonderful for teaching art to an older child. I used many of the activities with 5th and 6th graders with some astounding results.

MATH

Cuisenaire Rods. Cuisenaire rods are used in many schools around the country to introduce basic math concepts. Parents can send for a set of the rods to use at home. Ask for the "Math Made Meaningful" kit. It includes 155 rods, 50 topic cards, and an instructor's manual. The price as of the date of this book's publication is $23.95 for a set of plastic rods or $25.95 for a set of wooden rods. Add 8% of the amount for postage and handling. (You might want to call first to check on the prices.)

    Cuisenaire Co. of America
    12 Church Street, Box D
    New Rochelle, New York 10802
  Phone: (914) 235-0900

MUSIC

"Wee Sing" cassettes are wonderful! Price Stern & Sloan Inc. has also produced two videos—"Wee Sing Together" and "King Cole's Birthday"—both of which work children's songs into a story that is full of fun.

Sharon, Lois, and Bram is a trio that has wonderful records and cassettes, many of which include children singing along.

Walt Disney's "Sing Along Songs" videos offer exerpts from Disney classics with songs such as "Whistle While You Work" from *Snow White* and "The Siamese Cat Song" from *Lady and the Tramp.*

"A Gentle Wind" has a complete line of children's cassettes, both songs and story tapes. A favorite of mine is "My Rhinocerous and Other Friends", by Guy Carawan. For a free catalogue, write or call: A Gentle Wind, Box 3103, Albany, New York 12203. (518) 482-9023.

MAGAZINES

For parents: Save old issues to use ideas later that you and your child weren't ready for when the magazine was published. Both of the magazines listed below offer a wide variety of articles for parents with children from infants to junior high school.

Parents Magazine
Parenting

For Children (ages 2–5)
Chickadee Magazine
Highlights for Children
Humpty Dumpty's Magazine
Owl Magazine
Sesame Street Magazine
Turtle Magazine for Preschool Kids

TELEVISION

In most homes, the television set is on far too many hours, and most of us agree we could and should watch less. But to help make the time spent watching television a little more worthwhile, you can send for a booklet entitled "TV Tips for Parents: Using Television to Help Your Child Learn."

Send a self-addressed business-size envelope with 39¢ postage to:

The Corporation for Public Broadcasting
Dept. P.
P.O. Box 33039
Washington, D.C. 20033

FREE MANUALS FROM THE AMERICAN READING COUNCIL

The Council has prepared a series of manuals to help parents encourage their children (birth to teens) to become readers. While the Council stresses the danger of trying to push children to read, it explains the advantages of providing them with opportunities to learn.

The manuals are free. However, you may be asked later for a donation. To receive one or more of the manuals, write to:

The American Reading Council
45 John Street, Suite 811
New York, New York 10038

Include your name, address, the ages of your children, and $2.50 for postage and handling. Ask for "Help Your Child At Home to Become A Reader."

More good books from ✿ Williamson Publishing

PUBLIC SCHOOLS USA
A Comparative Guide to School Districts
by Charles Harrison

"How are the schools?" is the question most asked by families on the move whether its cross-town, cross-state or cross-country. Finally, here's the answer as over 500 school districts in major metropolitan areas nationwide are rated on everything from special programs for high- or low-achievers to SAT scores, to music and art programs, to drop-out rates. If your children's education matters to you, here's a book you'll want to own.

368 pages, 8 1/2 × 11
Quality paperback, $17.95.

Easy-to-Make
GIFTS FOR THE BABY
by Cindy Higgins

There's still nothing nicer than a home-crafted, straight from the heart, gift for babies and toddlers. Somehow store-bought just doesn't measure up. Here are 65 gifts—everything from practical carry-all totes to huggable bunnies and two-sided dolls to clever wooden toys, rocking chairs, clown book shelf, and toy soldier clothes racks. Plus quick and easy quilts, blankets, kids backpacks. Best of all—simple directions and many projects to make in an hour or less!

144 pages, 8 1/4 × 7 1/4, how-to illustrations
Quality paperback, $8.95

GOLDE'S HOMEMADE COOKIES
by Golde Hoffman Soloway

"Cookies are her chosen realm and how sweet a world it is to visit."
Publishers Weekly

Over 100 treasured recipes that defy description. Suffice it to say that no one could walk away from Golde's cookies without asking for another . . . plus the recipe.

144 pages, 8 1/4 × 7 1/4, illustrations
Quality paperback, $7.95.

PARENTING THROUGH THE COLLEGE YEARS
From Application Through Graduation
by Norman Giddan, Ph.D., and Sally Vallongo

Don't drop out when your kids go off to college! They may need you in a different capacity, but they need you just the same. Here's all about this amazing 4 years in the life of parents and their almost-adult children. A lifesaver in many, many ways!

192 pages, 6 × 9
Quality paperback, $9.95.

THE BROWN BAG COOKBOOK:
Nutritious Portable Lunches for Kids and Grown-Ups
by Sara Sloan

Here are more than 1,000 brown bag lunch ideas with 150 recipes for simple, quick, nutritious lunches that kids will love. Breakfast ideas, too!

192 pages, 8 1/4 × 7 1/4, illustrations
Quality paperback, $8.95.

BIKING THROUGH EUROPE:
A Roadside Travel Guide with 17 Planned Cycle Tours
by Dennis & Tina Jaffe

Imagine the most idyllic biking vacation in Euorpe, winding your way through the Bourdeaux region of France or on a 3-country (Germany, Austria, Switzerland) tour around Lake Constance, stopping at wonderful cafes and bakeries, picnicing at little known, out-of-the-way scenic treasures. All this and more can be your experience using the Jaffe's fabulous book jam-packed with detailed, specific information.

304 pages, 6 × 9, detailed maps, 20 outstanding tours
Quality paperback, $13.95.

DINING ON DECK: Fine Food for Sailing & Boating
by Linda Vail

For Linda Vail a perfect day's sail includes fine food—quickly and easily prepared. She offers here 225 outstanding recipes (casual yet elegant food) with over 90 menus for everything from elegant weekends to hearty breakfasts and suppers for cool weather sailing. Her recipes are so good and so varied you'll use her cookbook year-round for sure!

160 pages, 8 × 10, illustrated.
Quality paperback, $9.95.

AFTER COLLEGE
The Business of Getting Jobs
by Jack Falvey

Wise and wonderful . . . don't leave college without it. Filled with unorthodox suggestions (avoid campus recruiters at all costs!), hands-on tools (put your money in stationery, not in resumes), wise observations (Grad school?—why pay to learn what others are paid to learn better). You've already spent a fortune on textbooks. Now for only $10 you can have the most valuable book of all.

192 pages, 6 × 9
Quality paperback, $9.95

TO ORDER

At your bookstore or order directly from Williamson Publishing. We accept Visa or Mastercard (please include number, expiration date and signature), or send check to **Williamson Publishing Co., Church Hill Road, P.O. Box 185, Charlotte, Vermont 05445.** (Phone orders: 800-356-8791.) Please add $1.50 for postage and handling. Satisfaction guaranteed or full refund without questions or quibbles.